THE NOT SO BUTTONED-UP APPROACH

CHANDRIA HARRIS

Copyright © 2021 by Chandria Harris

All rights reserved.

No part of this book may be reproduced in any form or by any electronic or mechanical means, including information storage and retrieval systems, without written permission from the author, except for the use of brief quotations in a book review.

CONTENTS

Foreword   v

1. The White Buttoned Up   1
2. Congratulations   5
3. What is Calling You?   14
4. The Career Brand   29
5. Networking To The Next Level   44
6. The Story that Gets Hired   66
7. Landing The Dream Career   86
8. Must-Have Critical Skills   106
9. Show up and Show Out   118
10. You Have to Keep It Now   132
11. Succeeding with Grace   148
12. You Have Arrived   157

Testimonials   167
Acknowledgments   171
About the Author   175

FOREWORD

FOREWORD

As a soon-to-be or recent graduate, there are many situations that will be stressful: the job hunt process, the pressure to "gain experience," to make connections, to work your internship, to figure out how to start paying your student loans while also taking on your first car loan. It feels like these things all happen suddenly, and coincidentally at the same time - the first practical exercise in balance for the newly-minted adult.

To make matters even more chaotic, it's also the first time you're told "Good luck!" with little to no backup plan. Just the act of figuring out what to wear to your first interview is stressful, let alone the anxiety to write a perfect resume, hone your interview skills, and oftentimes, apply for dozens of jobs without a

FOREWORD

single response back. It's a competitive market out there, and sometimes starting your career right after graduation can make you vulnerable to all the uncertainty there is surrounding it.

Chandria Harris to the rescue. She shoots it to you straight, makes you do the work, and demonstrates how you can show confidence, strength, and dignity in this incredibly vulnerable time. Her years of career coaching place you a step ahead, and you get one more perk too. As an African American woman, Chandria gets what this world is like for millennials, first-generation graduates, and diverse jobseekers.

What Chandria proves time and time again is that the career coaching websites, online services, and books of the past don't necessarily demonstrate what a job search is like for millennials. After all, how is someone near retirement supposed to know what the entry-level industry is like these days? Even the job search process from a decade ago is different from what it is now. Chandria understands the ins and outs of this process from both the employer and the candidate side.

To get what you want out of this book, you will need to do the work. You will need to reflect, actually do the exercises listed, and figure out who *you* are. The black skirt, white button-up approach does not work for everyone, so determine what makes *you* marketable. You are your own brand, and it is okay to be different as long as you make that difference count.

FOREWORD

The truth is, while Chandria speaks to the first-generation, often diverse populations of soon-to-be/recent graduates, her experience of finding the perfect buttoned-up shirt for her first real interview is not remarkable. In fact, what's so beautiful about her story is that it showcases her strength, her proactivity, her flexibility and her resiliency. All characteristics that are sought after by employers over and over again.

If you follow her guidance, you will inevitably reach success. But don't be afraid to take your time. Don't be afraid to think deeply. Don't be afraid to care greatly. This is your career at stake. This is your livelihood. For some, this will be your identity. Follow her direction, put yourself out there, and be intentional about every choice you make. But be sure to enjoy the journey.

1

THE WHITE BUTTONED UP

I was taking my last few summer classes to complete my graduation requirements, while working two different jobs. I'd saved up a couple hundred dollars, and one afternoon I dragged my mom and my sister to one of my favorite department stores so that I could get the perfect interview suit.

I already knew what I needed to pick out to wear, the universal attire every professional person I've ever spoken to told me to wear. A white buttoned-up shirt, tucked in, underneath a black blazer. A skirt and a comfortable black pair of pumps, complimented by the most befitting pantyhose to complete the look.

I arrived to the department store on a hot, humid June afternoon in Mississippi and I started gathering items to try on in the dressing room. I tried on my pencil skirt, and stuffed the white buttoned-up into the waist of my skirt.

I remember thinking, "Why does this feel so stiff?" Every time I lifted my arms, the whole shirt came untucked, not to mention it looked like the buttons could burst at any moment. Maybe I should go up a size?

"Mom! Nisha, grab me a men's shirt size 14 in the white oxford shirt!"

She came back, I tried it on, and looked in the mirror. The shirt was too long, and the point at the shoulder-seam made me look like I was wearing shoulder pads. Even still, the shirt's buttons were about to burst at the chest-- although perhaps slightly less so. The look on my mom's face showed that she definitely agreed. After trying on all of the white oxford shirts in the store, both men's and women's, I was practically in tears, ready to leave the store entirely. But my mom stepped in.

"Chan, I know your counselors, sorority advisors, professors and all these people told you to come into this store and buy a white button-up shirt and a black skirt, but baby you were blessed like mama," She pointed to her own chest. "You will not be able to fit this shirt. It wasn't made for people who are top-heavy like us. We need to look for a different shirt. It can still be white, Chandria, but you're not going to be able to wear this button-up."

Voice cracking, I managed to say, "Okay, Ma. Let's look for a different shirt."

Extremely frustrated, I assisted my mom and sister

with finding a different shirt for me, but in my head, I needed that white buttoned-up shirt! From magazines, tv shows, and Cosmopolitan articles, research shows, it is important to look a certain way. And now I was going to my first big interview lacking the one thing everyone said I needed.

Frustrated with my moping, my Mom pulled me into the dressing room again and had a couple words for me. "Chandria, you have always been different. Don't allow that white button-up shirt to stop you from celebrating getting that interview. You have always been unique Chandria. Please, just try on something else. Wear something different."

I knew she was right. Whatever I'd been told, I had to pick out and buy a different type of shirt, if not out of physical necessity, for the person I knew myself to be. Up to this point, I'd never been the type of girl who did what everyone else did. I'd always had a little extra sass in me. When I was told to wear a certain color, dress, attire, I'd always put my little spin to it.

Being different is my thing, and even as I prepared for interviews, it became abundantly clear that I had to own my difference.

I walked out of the store that day having purchased a shimmery white v-neck blouse with two little buttons at the top. It was beautiful. It showed personality. It fit me.

Fast forward to a couple months later, and that white buttoned-up shirt was foreshadowing for the job search ahead. After countless applications, and days and days of effort, the traditional routes weren't working—just like that white buttoned-up shirt. I knew I had to do something different.

So, I did.

2

CONGRATULATIONS

For hours, I sat in my living room and pondered the thoughtful words of encouragement expressed to me from my parents, my siblings, mentors, family and friends.

"You will go far, Chandria!"

"If anyone in the family can do it, it's you!"

"You have what it takes!"

And my personal favorite...

"You have your whole family counting on you, we know you can do it!"

My mom cried tears of joy. My dad looked into my eyes and told me that this was one of his proudest moments. My baby sister smiled from ear to ear. My little brothers played way too much. My aunts' hugs, kisses and warmth. And me, basking in my glory. "I have graduated," I thought.

"I have arrived."

Confidently enough, I believed I would go places, but to where? I believed I had what it takes, but what did I really know? My whole family was depending on me—that's a lot of nerve-wrecking pressure!

Looking back, I truly believed I would go far in my career... but the first step was hard. From finding the perfect outfit for interviews, to landing interviews, it was a struggle. Like you, reading this book right now, I didn't know how or where to start. Instead, I was left sitting in my living room for hours, trying to map my career plan, a plan that would make my family and me so very proud. But I had no idea where to begin.

Let's be real.

You don't have to be from a city with unlimited career opportunities or department stores. You don't have to be equipped with unlimited professional development programs to prepare for the working world.

I'm from the friendly city of Columbus, Mississippi. Yes, Mississippi. With a whopping population of less than 25,000 people and even fewer while I was growing up there. We have one Wal-Mart, one hospital, one department store, one city high school and about 4 main occupations: education, healthcare, large manufacturing/industrial, and retail. That is it!

My hometown is full of love, food, and family, but none of the career opportunities I dreamt of. No major corporate opportunities. No skyline. No huge internship opportunities. No major business programs for high school or college students. It is truly a retirement town.

So, there I was, finally having graduated, embarking

on my career journey. I had limited to no financial resources, a whole world of connections out there that I thought I had absolutely no link to, and the added pressure of making my family, friends and community back home proud. Being the first to do everything comes with very little instruction. The only guidance I ever received was to "go far", "be successful", "wear a white buttoned up shirt and black skirt with a blazer to your interviews", and "work hard and everything will work out!" Great motivational words, but not exactly the step-by-step directions I was looking for, or needed.

Eight long years of adventure later —with lots of love, a couple of huge mess-ups and thankfully, many moments of success —I'm in the Music City (260 miles from my hometown) living in my brand new home, with a wonderful husband, a wonderful career and an adventurous baby boy. Before the baby boy, I lived smack in the middle of Nashville's bachelorette-filled, music-centric Broadway with the hubby. I'm am the first person in my family to obtain a Bachelor's Degree, to obtain a Master's Degree, and to graduate and move to another city. I am the first person in my family who has even attempted to land a corporate job and the first to ever live in a city of over 30,000 people.

Building this new life wasn't an overnight process. For a while, I lived off of minimum wage and student loans chasing a dream. I worked for temporary agencies to gain internship experience because I struggled with landing an internship. I made it through knowing how to utilize the limited connections I had starting conversations that eventually landed me bigger networks and career opportunities. I worked traditional 9-5 opportunities while taking night courses. I lost an important scholarship after moving all of my classes online when my Mom got sick.

I made it through, and as you think about yourself and your struggles, I have good news for you: You will make it, too. You can identify your career calling, fall in love with yourself while developing your brand, get connected to decision makers (even if you currently have none), and land the job of your dreams. Most importantly, you can fulfill your life's mission to be great and to help people. I am here to show you how.

I came from love, lots of prayer, and a dream to help my family and that was just enough to push me to be the award-winning career global career consultant, diversity champion, thought influencer I am today. I have dedicated my entire career to helping people discover financial freedom and a life worth living by identifying and outlining the way to get to their highest career success. I have both seen and been a person who lands a job interview within thirty minutes of applying to a job. I have both seen and been a person who gets the job just thirty minutes after interviewing. I have seen clients bounce back from a nasty termination and a failed business venture. I have helped thousands of ambitious students land career opportunities from Rolls Royce, to the Pentagon, to Google, and I am going to help you too!

If I can do it—if these clients can do it—you have no excuses.

I know the feeling that you need to give up on your dreams. It can feel like the weight of the world is on your shoulders. One of the greatest responsibilities for a first-generation college student is to successfully stay on top of everything that is going on in life, and continuing to prepare for the future. Our 24-hour days are consumed with 8:00 a.m. phone calls from home discussing what happened last night, to the emergency situation that came up this morning, to managing all five class syllabi, all while trying to work and send money back home to help with the bills.

Day by day life happens, until all of a sudden you are about to graduate and you haven't even sat down to think about *your* future. Shit happens! Shit always happens, especially when you feel like you have exhausted all of your resources and you are doing all that you can do. It's easy to procrastinate on your dreams, and pick the tasks that are much easier to accomplish. But that doesn't mean you should give up.

After coaching second-generation clients, I have learned that it's hard for them as well. To follow in the footsteps of successful parents is difficult. I have seen clients who battle with anxiety because of daily talks with their parents about what they think they should do next.

They are not only micromanaged by their successful parents, but they may also be stressed about financial burdens or new responsibilities. They're also worried that if they mess up, they're on their own, and they'll never be successful without ties to their family. They experience pressure, stress, and still little to no real guidance. And just as it's easy for first-generation students to be overwhelmed by the life getting in the way of their dreams. It's easy for second generation students to just say forget it all and fall in line.

I would have never thought that buying my interview attire would be a defining moment in my life and career. I tried to follow the step-by-step guide created for professionals to get a head start in life. Although highly recommended, universal, and some would say the best shirt to wear to an interview, it didn't fit me. Neither did finding an amazing job posting, applying to the job, and waiting for an interview. Neither did the networking advice I received as a new graduate, the chorus of "Call your favorite aunt who is an attorney, a cousin who is a doctor, uncle who is an engineer, and tell them to connect you with their networks."

The white buttoned-up shirt may not work for everyone. It is okay to be different as long as you make that difference marketable and uniquely you.

That's where this book comes in. You'll learn a different approach to navigate your career journey.

For years, I searched up and down, high and low for a book that would help me. I needed a book that would teach me everything I wanted to know to start my career. I needed a grey area guideline, not just the black-and-white traditional knowledge about starting a career, but a resource that will tie everything together. I had the energy, the drive, enthusiasm, but very little resources to get me kickstarted. I created this guide because I wished someone had given me something like it. I want to provide other young ambitious professionals with the resources I needed as I first navigated the workforce.

It's a step-by-step guide for you to read and apply immediately starting with chapter one.

Each chapter is special and crafted to help you wherever you are in your career journey. You will go from learning how to identify your career calling, to crafting your career portfolio, to landing the career opportunity, and keeping that job!

In "What is Calling You," you will gather a sense of career identity. This chapter will help you discover your career calling and empower you to commit to making your mark in this world. It will dare you to prepare for your wildest career dreams and offer thought-provoking questions to help you assess where you are and where you would like to be.

In "The Best Kept Secret," you will explore how to brand yourself for your career. We all have a gift that only a few know about, and this chapter will help you to define your gifts and bring them out for the world.

In "Networking To The Next Level," you will be

provided with step-by-step directions to get connected to some of the most powerful leaders in your community or the world. I will guide you on connecting with the powerful, and help you prove to them why they should work with you!

In "The Story That Gets Hired," you will learn how to catch the attention of recruiters and your potential boss. You will learn how to craft a well-written resume, create a compelling cover letter, and beat the applicant tracking system. Your story is what will get you hired every time, and this chapter will further tell you how to share it!

In "Landing Your Dream Career," you will be taught the tricks and techniques to interview like the CEO. Interviewing is an art and it is very easy to do once you have mastered an understanding of the company. The dream job will soon become a reality once you have finished this chapter.

In "Must-Have Critical Skills," I will provide you in detail the characteristics companies look for most in a candidate. These critical skills are a must and in everything you do, you must be able to demonstrate them.

In "Show Up & Show Out," we talk about leveling up. We sometimes wonder how some people get promoted and others don't. Well, worry no more because in this chapter you will explore healthy habits that will not only get you hired, but also get you promoted and get you paid.

In "Keeping The Job Is Harder," we will explore the

unprofessional workplace habits that send so many people out the door with one box in hand. Getting fired is real and ruins reputations, so I wanted to be sure to share with you tips that keep you safe!

Finally, you have arrived. Although, you will go through situations, circumstances, and bad breaks, you will conquer.

I had to go through crazy career moments. A period of transition working with temporary agencies. A moment or two of financial struggle to put together a piece of work that could help the next person. Here it is. I hope it guides you to your wildest dreams. I hope it activates your confidence, stir up your gifts and pushes you to your destiny! Congratulations and let's get started.

3

WHAT IS CALLING YOU?

Skipping the struggle is not an option for most people, so go ahead and struggle your way to success.

In an era of social media, we feel like we are very connected to so many amazing people who have their Sh!t together. It amazes me how we're able to extract just a portion of our life in a way that allows us to portray to others a story we want to share. Be it the whole truth or not. Since everyone "seems" to have their sh!t together by their mid-twenties, it makes people like you and me feel like we are doing things all wrong.

We get so invested in these individual's stories: their fame, their clothes, their careers, and their influence, that we purchase their products with hopes that they will magically turn our life into a success story. Just like theirs.

Now, I'm not saying that all influencers are taking

advantage, but most of the secrets, techniques, "get more followers" stuff is really a fraud. If you look at their full biography (which most won't show), the reality is that it has taken *years* for them to build their current following and success.

So now, the ball is back in your court after paying thousands of dollars brunching with the best, hiring and taking coaching calls with the most influential people you can find, and praying every night that something comes through. I'm going to be totally honest with you when I say this, unless you are a Kardashian or a child of many inheritances, skipping the struggle is not an option for most people.

So go ahead and struggle your way to success.

What does that mean? When I say struggle your way to success, I mean begin the process of taking control of your own life. Get off Instagram, Facebook, Twitter, LinkedIn, and take time to get to know who you really are, and how you will change the world. Your gifts and talents were given to you for a reason and the world needs you to be great.

We often use the statement "be great" loosely. We use it in the completion of tasks. We feel like we have already changed the world and should be placed in our deserved office doing what we want to do and telling people what to do.

Not so fast, though. This will require some deep introspective thinking, writing, analyzing and assessing. Many times, we only have a vague idea of what we like to do, but not a name for the job. This is why, as a career coach, I highly recommend my clients take some time, gather their thoughts, and listen to their hearts when it comes to identifying what they would really like to do in this world.

Wanting it bad enough, is not enough.

Let me tell you about one of my clients, named "Brian," for confidentiality.

Brian reached out to me extremely excited about the prospect of finding an amazing career opportunity in Sales/Operations. He paid the retainer fee, set up his coaching calls, and waited patiently for me to respond to his application. When I called, he was extremely excited and eager to get started.

Almost too ready.

During our first session, he said, "Mrs. Harris, whatever you think I will be good at, just let me know. Give me the word, and I will go do it."

I told him candidly, "I don't tell people what to do. I help people find out what they would like to do."

Brian said, "Okay, I understand."

The next coaching session, he proved he didn't understand what I meant. At all.

The first thing he said in this second meeting was, "Based off what you know about me, write down three jobs with high paying salaries for me to choose from, and we will be done with our coaching sessions."

I was surprised. I had made it very clear that wasn't

what I did, and that I couldn't tell him what his future should be.

Brian sat back in his seat, put one leg over the other one and began to bounce them. He said, "You see, I am very easy to work with."

I told him, "No, you want me to do your work for you."

He looked at me with fire in his eyes and replied, "Yes, because I want it so bad!"

"What do you want so badly?"

"Money. I can see it! Big house, nice car, luxury trips, luxury dinners, taking care of my family members and even giving some of it to the homeless. I need some damn money."

I told him we all need money, but the way he was trying to get it wasn't necessarily going to come to you as fast as he thought. I went on to say that to get the money he was dreaming about, you are going to have to provide a service, an impact that absolutely needs to move their business goals forward. As an example, all small business owners need a fantastic accountant. All companies need a great website designer. All companies need a badass recruiter.

Long story short, Brian and I identified temporary placement opportunities for him to make money, and we are currently working on the master plan to his dream career.

I share this story because I believe many of you may know a "Brian"... Or maybe even you have "Brian" tendencies. You look around at these successful people and influencers on TV, in the community, and on social media and are interested in the "quick success" and money that they have.

The good news is the money you desire will become more available to you the moment you decide to answer your higher leadership and work calling. The bad news is, it doesn't happen overnight, and it definitely doesn't happen by accident.

Answering to your higher leadership and work calling will require you to fully embrace fear and run into the arms of success. Success is in the eye of the beholder and no one should set the record of success for you, except you. Your success should not be defined by what others think you should be doing. This can be tricky to navigate; you will and should consult your mentors, family, and friends about your values and strengths. However, they should not be the sole decision maker in your career success. That can only be you.

Sometimes, that can take a while to learn, which leads to yet another obstacle: It's easy for young professionals to get so caught up on time.

We want to make an impact, but we want to know exactly how long it will take to acquire a new skill, study for the exam, and fully complete the degree. If the timing isn't right, we become less and less interested. But you must consider the aspect of time. Don't let it become the roadblock that prevents you from moving forward towards your goal.

Another client, "Ashley," came to me for coaching to begin the process of answering her higher leadership and work calling. We were going through the career discovery section and she mentioned to me her interest in becoming a doctor, but was discouraged by how long it would actually take her to complete school. We discussed how long it usually takes someone to complete medical school and she screamed, "8-10 years? That's a *very* long time to be in school!"

Now, to individuals who are eager to save lives, 8-10 years may not sound so bad. And if you really consider the financial gain of becoming a physician, the idea to travel this route may sound even better. The truth is, you will have to struggle your way to success, anyway. So you might as well go ahead and decide to do what you would love to do!

When you decide to answer higher leadership and work calling, you give yourself permission to create a sustainable life that keeps your end goals in mind. Many young professionals identify success with having the means to fly across the country with their friends and having the income to do so, which is why they want money fast.

When you decide to answer your higher leadership and work calling, you give yourself permission to grow, share what you know, and watch your world thank you for your contribution.

When you decide to answer your higher leadership and work calling, you give yourself permission to dream, to believe bigger than you and to see magic happen in your life.

When you decide to answer your higher leadership and work calling, you have decided to not only live life, but contribute to others' lives... and then my friend, you allow money to flow to you abundantly!

Now go grab a pen, because I'm going to assist you with beginning the process of answering higher leadership and work calling. Write directly in this book and mark the pages with your dreams.

Before we move forward, I want you to understand that this will take time. You will need to make time and use the time you made wisely. But if you follow these instructions carefully and thoroughly, you will leave this chapter with resources to guide you on this journey toward success.

IN THIS SESSION, you will "Get to Know More About You".

Successful professionals often have a career identity. It's the image you see and hear about and possibly want to be like.

Career Identity: Career Identity is strategically structuring meaning in your life's work that encapsulates your desires, career interests, motivation, and innate talents. The first step in answering your higher leadership and work calling is to identify who you are and how you would like to change the world. This step is exhilarating because it allows you to dream and this phase of discovery will teach you about your innate abilities

Your Career Identity is made up of your vision for success (your career interests), your innate talents (things you naturally do well), your life's mission (your "Why") and your life's objective (how you plan to deliver your "why")

Understanding your career identity requires you to explore, dream, research and analyze your findings.

STEP #1: EXPLORING THE DREAM

Exercise: #1. How would you like to be remembered?

Let's plan your retirement party.

You are at the end of your career and amazing people are lined up and ready to receive an invitation to your retirement party.

Tell me all about it: Who gets an invitation? How does the room look? Are their affluent people there? What are people saying to you? Do you have children? Is your partner there?

Now tell me, why are all these people celebrating you? What did you do for them to come so far to celebrate with you? How did you do what you do? Who lives did you impact? Did you create something the world can't live without? What industry will miss you and why? How would you like for the world to remember you?

After you open your eyes from dreaming about this, answer each of the above questions on paper.

Exercise #2. The Job Description

What do you want your annual salary to be? Don't be shy…. Write down the truth. Now, tell me what you would do for the entire year to be compensated for the salary you wrote down. What would you do each month? Is there a certain city/state you would like to do this work in? Who would benefit from your services the most? What industry? List 5 responsibilities you would like to have while doing this job.

Exercise #3. Leveling Up

Since you have identified the job responsibilities you would like to have, now share with me what type of education, certification, degrees you will need. How long will it take for you to go to school? Look up job titles on Indeed or Glassdoor and find opportunities that match the responsibilities you are seeking. Now look down at the requirement section and tell me what type of experience you will need. How many years of experience are typical for this type of job? What benchmarks do you need to achieve prior to holding this position?

Exercise #4. Money Research

We now know the responsibilities you would like to have and what job title(s) you would like to hold... So now let's see if it's worth it. Research the industry you would like to go into. Google the highest paying jobs in the industry, then identify the entry level salary, middle management salary, high level salary. What cities/states hold the most job opportunities for the titles you are seeking? Think about your average salary opportunity for each year: Is this money worth the struggle? Will this portion of your salary supplement 75% of the average income you seek to make?

Exercise 5: Assessing the Dream

Let's take a look at what you're naturally good at. Below are a couple of assessments you should take to review your innate abilities. Take any of them and write about your findings. Assessments will serve a supplementary resource that will either confirm your dream, or provide you with insight on other opportunities to look into. Either way, the resource will reveal to you amazing characteristics about yourself!

ASSESSMENTS:

Myers-Briggs -- Personality assessment that will tell you more about your personality and how you would behave in certain environments, how to deal with people and your perception of others.

Kudor Journey – Career Inventory assessment that will share with you career interests, industries, work values and things you would be naturally confident doing in the workplace.

16 personalities.com – Personality assessment that will share with you your strengths, weaknesses, workplace environment needs, and careers you may be interested in.

Gallup Strengthsfinder – A mixture of a career inventory assessment and personality assessment that will share your top 5 strengths and how to leverage them in the workplace. This assessment will give you the language you need to speak with recruiters and decision makers about your strengths and how they will be beneficial in the workplace.

After assessing the dream, you must take all this information and put together a realistic Action Plan. How would you like to carry out your vision?

How long will it take, and what resources will you need to get there?

This is the stage where most people want to give up. The dreaming phase is fun, but when it comes time to create an Action Plan, living the dream can suddenly seem hard. This is also the stage where you can give yourself a little push and begin the work that allows you to live the life of your dreams.

One thing I have learned in my 20-something years of living is that life is all about balance and the output (what manifests and what you see is largely due to your input). You'll have to give so much to get exactly what you want. You will meet with a congratulations let's interview email and don't get the job. Moments of happiness and moments of sadness You can take risks or you can be mediocre. You can be happy living a rich life or you can be happy while earning the bare minimum. It is all up to you 100%.

That's why this is key: At the core of your life and career decisions, be sure to fall in love with finding success your way. Life is what you make it and answering higher leadership and work calling will be a responsibility of your own.

So, don't expect anyone to do the work for you. Don't expect anyone to be excited about your vision more than you. Don't expect anyone to welcome you with open arms to your rightful place. You will have to earn it and that is the struggle. Earn your education, your experience, and your reasoning for "Why" you deserve a seat at the table with decision makers. Don't allow time, your friends' decisions, your family's opinions, or social media to rush you or make you believe you are not moving fast enough. Enduring until you have reached your optimal level of success should be your ultimate goal.

Now you have step-by-step techniques to move you toward your higher leadership and work calling. But you must be very intentional about your next steps. Surround yourself with people in your industry who are working toward goals similar to yours. Network with professionals who are already champions in your career field. And don't forget to identify strategies that will assist you in coping with stress.

Now, create a vision board and get to work!

With my first recommendation, I'm not telling you to let go of your old friends. I am recommending that you gather a core group of advisors in your industry who will be able to answer questions for you along the way.

Unless your friend group is filled with professionals in your industry, you will have to block out their well-meaning but unsolicited advice and seek out sound, proven, and educated advice from professionals in your industry.

Here's an example: I once had a client who was one year behind in college because she listened to her friend who told her not to take a class.

You know how it is. She put her courses in a GroupMe and someone recommended that she not take a class from a particular professor. She knew she needed the class to move forward with graduating on time, however, she decided she would wait and take the class the next semester when another professor was available.

This ended up being the worst decision of her college career. When she went to enroll in the class the next semester, she found out the class she needed to graduate would not be available until the following spring semester! And of course, only one professor teaches it... the one she tried to avoid in the first place!

Just like you wouldn't go to your hair stylist and ask them to give you a massage, don't rely on your friends to give you industry advice. The process is progress. When someone tells you about their challenges, understand one thing: Their challenge is not yours. Listen, evaluate, thank them for sharing, and make a mental note, but do not use it to drive your decision-making process.

Answering your higher leadership and work calling is a journey towards developing your career success. It will be filled with small wins that will soon add up to your big dreams in reality-form. Step-by-step and day-by-day is the only way you will be able to accomplish all the goals you have set out for yourself. Consider it giving yourself CPR: Be Consistent, Persistent, and Resilient. We both understand that this process may be a little nerve-wracking and scary but J.Cole said it best, "If you allow fear to kill your dreams, it will haunt you".

The world is full of bitter people who decided not to move forward with their dreams and they are the very people who are giving advice, alternative ideas, and negative energy. Protect your heart and protect your dreams just like you protect or will protect your children. Fall in love with reading the right sh!t that will motivate you every day. As Zig Ziglar said, "People often say that motivation doesn't last. Well, neither does bathing—that's why we recommend it daily."

My call to action is for you to join me and thousands of other professionals who struggled to succeed and live the life of your dreams.

As I said earlier, when you decide to answer your higher leadership and work calling, you give yourself permission to create a sustainable life that is long lasting, not just a quick trip with your friends across the country.

When you decide to answer your higher leadership and work calling, you give yourself permission to grow, share what you know, and watch your world thank you for your contribution.

When you decide to answer your higher leadership and work calling, you give yourself permission to dream, to believe bigger and to see magic happen in your life.

When you decide to answer you higher leadership and work calling, you have decided to not only live life, but contribute to the lives of others and then my friend, you have decided to allow money to flow to you abundantly!

4

THE CAREER BRAND

Don't Wait For the Perfect Moment. Take The Moment and Make It Perfect – Unknown

Figuring out who you are as a young professional is hard. But keep this in mind... the moment you have a semblance of the thought, "this is who I am" is the exact moment you begin building your career brand. You are already dedicating yourself to answering your higher career calling. You are already committing to impacting the world by using your skills and solving a specific problem. Next, you must figure out how to make others understand your purpose.

The key to establishing an impactful and influential career brand is to identify what knowledge you have gained that will offer expert solutions to problems in your industry.

For example, my friend Riley is a great writer. In college, all of her professors used to comment on her essays, brag and boast to the class about how talented she was. She aced her writing assignments and was happy to serve as editor of all of her friends' papers. She majored in Communications and enjoyed helping to critiquing her church members' letters, important emails and correspondences. Her goal was to one day become a book publishing editor, but she didn't know exactly how to get her career brand started.

We turned her "one day" goal to her current side hustle by sharing with others her talents and marketing her strengths online. Within months, Riley went from looking for the perfect moment to become an editor to having a full-time schedule editing academic research papers!

In this chapter, we'll discuss how to brand your career in a way that moves people to hire you to do the job!

When it comes to establishing an impactful and influential career brand you must know what your skills are, identify what makes you special, and properly share with the world your strengths.

Skills

Getting hired to complete a job is less challenging when someone knows for a fact that you can do the job successfully. But you must be certain that you can do the job successfully. You must hire yourself first, knowing that you are confident, proficient and amazing at the work you want to do!

Whether you are looking for freelance work, or to work with a company or organization, the same rules apply. Everybody will demand experience. Experience is a prerequisite to landing freelance opportunities or landing that VP position. Hell, it's even critical to landing entry-level opportunities. Literally everything requires some form of experience. So, no matter what, you must be prepared to answer the question, "What experience do you have to do this work successfully?"

I'm going to take you way back to how I got my start writing resumes.

One thing all of my friends can confidently tell you is that Chandria has always kept a job. I was joking with one of my girlfriends one day and she said to me, "Girl, you always have a job, Chan. Help me with my resume."

It was that moment when I realized... I was kind of good at writing resumes. I did it to help my friends and college students land jobs, and when I started, I wrote them for free. Anybody who wanted a job and said out loud, "But I need to update my resume," I was the first person to raise my hand and help out.

After I revamped a few resumes for family and friends, they began to land interviews. I was so excited! I began to learn more about different resume styles, for different fields of work. I began to practice writing different types of resumes, and I quickly found out how easily this skill came to me.

Around the same time, as my friends began to graduate, they helped to spread the word about me and the rest was history. I started my business of writing resumes and charging a fee. After a while, I didn't want to just be a resume writer. I wanted to be really good at it. I looked into certifications, went after those certifications, earned those certifications, and upped my prices! This happened over and over until I realized it was time to offer more services. Before long, my dream of career coaching started to take off.

You see, everyone starts out as a Rookie. It is okay to be a beginner, so long as you are doing what it takes to get better. Everyone will be entry-level, no one really can skip this step. You must gain additional skills if you seek to elevate your career to a higher level.

The smartest thing you can do is to begin today by gaining experience and strengthening your skills. Once you have done this, opportunity is sure to follow.

Now, I am going to say something that might scare you, and it might be a little controversial. It is okay to do an internship for no financial benefit, if you have never had an internship before. Sometimes the benefit is wrapped in the exposure and access.

It's not forever, and in many cases, it's the foot in the door that you need to be selected for bigger and better internships at bigger and better companies. It is also okay to continue an internship after you have graduated (although, not for forever!). Sometimes, getting those high-level opportunities will require you to take on things that others are not willing to do. When you accept things others are not willing to do, you will land opportunities others are not qualified for because you have both the grit and experience.

The number one thing you must do is embody the skills needed to get the job done.

Value Proposition

When an employer asks you, "Tell me about yourself."

When an employer asks you, "Why should we pick you?"

When an employer asks, "Why should we pick you over the other candidate?"

You must be prepared to say why you are special. Everyone has something that makes them special, the better choice over other candidates. You must identify why you deserve to land the gig. Wanting it bad, being hard-working, being organized, or being patient will not be enough information. You must know exactly why you are special, why you deserve the opportunity, and why you are the best person for the job.

This is your Value Proposition.

There is a never-ending list of professionals who are great at writing resumes and coaching professionals to success. Trust me, I have done the research!

They are certified by the same associations as I am, with advanced degrees, and experience working for amazing companies. What makes me special?

I'm an African-American Woman and a first-generation graduate. I relate to the younger generation, because I am a member of that generation. I have inside knowledge into young professionals' desires.

That being said, I've also sat on the other side of the table. I have served in Human Resources and know the inside scoop on what skills and traits employers seek the most. And because I have experience on both sides, I am able to help companies to marry the two. I am able to bring our generational insight into corporate America. And I am also able to help companies retain millennial employees, utilize their strengths, and facilitate a company culture that finds value and compromise in both sides. That is my value proposition, and it is something I never leave an interview without portraying.

Your Value Proposition is the strengths, benefits, and solutions that you are able to deliver to the company or client. They are your struggles, your triumphs, your story, your education, your history, your ambition, and most importantly your "why." All of these things create a story, and combined will help you create an amazing value proposition that will bring hiring managers to tears! It will get you hired on the spot, and promoted to positions you never dreamed possible.

Allow your compelling story of determination to add flavor, life, and enthusiasm to your value proposition. Then, when a prospective employer asks you that famous line, "Tell me a little about yourself," you are already equipped to share with them your story, your skills, your triumphs, and how these relate to the job you're about to get.

As the first person in my family to graduate, they rely on me a lot to speak up for them. One of my favorite childhood memories is when I negotiated with my grandmother's property owner the best times for her to pay her rent. I was no more than 10 years old.

The property owner called and I heard my grandmother murmur, "I can't pay it today."

I said, "Grandmother when do you think you can pay it?"

She smiled and said. "On friday."

The phone rang again shortly after our conversation. I picked up and told the property owner that my grandmother could pay her bill on friday, and fridays are usually better for her.

It worked! My granny called my mom laughing uncontrollably while she shared how I was able to get Mr. Carter to change her rent. From that moment on, I have been known in the family to speak up. Thank goodness my community allowed me to do this! Because of that, I truly believe they helped me to become a badass negotiator. Now, I confidently take on the toughest and most difficult conversations.

To this day negotiation, persuasion, communication, and presentations are my greatest strengths! Think about it. I have been practicing since I was eight years old! Not only have I gained the degrees, but I have the street credit and actual experience to negotiate for more! That is the type of career coach you want. Someone who will hold you accountable to get every dollar you deserve.

I say all of this to impress upon you a few key goals:

1. Identify what makes you special.
2. Shout that sh!t all over the world.

Your sweat, tears, experiences, triumphs, upsets and bad breaks have developed you to become the best in business and you owe it to yourself and others to let people know about it!

Now, this book is not just about telling you how to do things. I am a career coach, and coaches hold you accountable. I'm leaving you with some homework that will help you to identify your skills, find your value proposition, and thus, begin to build your career brand.

The Best Kept Secret

The only "best-kept secrets" I want in my life are my shoe collection and my perfume. When it comes to my abilities, my skills and my strengths, there are no secrets. I would like for the world to know.

No one would have ever known that my neighbor

was the best baker in our small town if she didn't start by making cupcakes for family and friends. No one would ever know my friend Katy is a great writer if she didn't start by doing it for free. No one would ever know how amazing I am at writing resumes if I kept procrastinating on starting my own. Long story short… stop being the best kept secret. It is now time to get noticed for the amazing work you do. People want to know about those who can take action and make a difference. How will they know you exist if you stay quiet?

In the age of technology, this isn't difficult. Display your skills and market them on every social media platform possible. Especially LinkedIn. Be a leader of thought and write a weekly article about your industry. When people post problems, offer up solutions. Get in touch and stay in touch with people in and adjacent to your industry. Share your value proposition in your LinkedIn summary. Update your accomplishment section and ask people you have worked with for recommendations. Act like an authority—because you are!

Work social media and allow social media to work for you. When my friend Katy wrote an article online about her new essay business, people went crazy. Her post went viral. At the end of the first day she had more than 50 shares, 1000 likes and an inbox full of clients interested in her business. She was completely blown away by the reaction.

I wasn't.

Katy edited papers and projects for free for many of her LinkedIn connections. They all felt compelled to help her with her new business, and they knew she was the real deal. The rest was history! Every week, Katy posted testimonials, former clients continued to write her recommendations, and her business continued to grow. It wasn't long before she received an email from an area principal asking if she could host a summer class for incoming high school seniors on how to write a college admissions essay.

Fast-forward a few years, Katy is no longer her hometown's best-kept secret. She has been featured in multiple magazines, blogs, and websites on essay writing in higher education. She is booked and busy, writing and working with students, and she is in love with her work.

When it comes to establishing an impactful and influential career brand, you must know what your skills are, identify what makes you special, and properly and professionally share with the world your strengths.

Just like me, Katy, my neighbor, and thousands of other professionals who have made their start, you can make your start too. You are so special, and the world needs you to be great.

Your talents can be showcased during an interview, just as much as you can advertise them on social media. Bring your skills, knowledge, solutions and ideas to the table and they will have no choice but to hire you. The goal is to craft your responses to exemplify how you will be able to handle the tasks and responsibilities in this role. Display your latest knowledge, be able to problem solve, know what the position requires, and you will be rewarded for your efforts.

Don't wait for the perfect moment to get started making a name for yourself! This is your moment. Start today doing something that will move your career endeavors forward. You are the author of your dreams and the mover of your faith. Everything happens for you and with you when you decide to strengthen your skills and serve the world.

EXERCISE

Record your answers within this book!

Step #1: Talk to the people in your life who have known you since you were a child. Ask them to tell you stories about your childhood. What is one strength they noticed you have had since you were a child? What problems do they think you solve naturally? Record their answers here.

Step #2: Take inventory of your ambitions and everything you like to do. Nothing is too small.

1. What are you naturally gifted at and how do you know?

   _____
   _____
   _____
   _____

2. If you could be someone to help solve any problem in this world, what problem would you like to solve?

   _____
   _____
   _____
   _____

3. Write down times you have struggled and how you have overcome your trials

   _____
   _____
   _____
   _____

EXERCISE

Record your answers within this book!

Step #1: Talk to the people in your life who have known you since you were a child. Ask them to tell you stories about your childhood. What is one strength they noticed you have had since you were a child? What problems do they think you solve naturally? Record their answers here.

Step #2: Take inventory of your ambitions and everything you like to do. Nothing is too small.

4. Now, tell yourself what you are good at. Write down education, certifications or classes you can take that can help you get better at it.

   _____
   _____
   _____
   _____

5. Who are the people doing what you would like to do?

   _____
   _____
   _____
   _____

5

NETWORKING TO THE NEXT LEVEL

Education and experience alone are not good enough in today's candidate market - in most cases, your most effective tool will be your network. Building your network can begin at any time; the first thing you'll need is somebody who knows what you have to offer. As hard as it may seem to some, networking begins with building an authentic relationship with a professional who is willing to connect you to your next level.

It's what I call dating at its finest. You have to meet professionals, get to know them, find out how you can serve them and then communicate your willingness to be an asset in their lives. Networking takes time, energy, money, love, sweat and most importantly authentic relationships. Your life will be transformed during the process!

When you think of networking, you might picture

attending events and passing out business cards. But while this seems like the most popular way to connect with people, it's actually looked down upon by professionals who are actually relational. Attending events is only one form of networking, after all, and in this chapter we will discuss several forms of networking and how to tap into the hidden market of networking to get you to the next level of your success.

The most authentic and genuine way to network is to lose yourself in serving others. Passion and purpose drives placement and promotions, and when you serve an organization with compassion and utilize your supreme purpose in the process, somebody will see you, talk about you, promote you, help you, and get you to the next level. Don't be afraid to volunteer your time and talents by providing services to an individual or organization for free.

The key is to begin this networking process before you actually need the job. Networking naturally takes time. You can't volunteer for an hour one month and expect someone to gauge your skills and your personality enough to put their own credibility on the line. Word-of-mouth is the best marketing, and although it seems like nothing, in reality it is everything.

Think about it like this: Most decisions about your career are made when you are not in the room. These opportunities only arise because people are speaking positively about your ability to handle projects, tasks, vision, and your work ethic. You won't even be there to promote yourself! Remember, it is always better to take a call from someone who wants something from you, than for you to make a call and ask someone for that opportunity.

Volunteering allows you to strengthen your skills and serve someone simultaneously. By volunteering, you will receive exposure and connect with other professionals who enjoy working for the same cause. This network of volunteers will likely be or know of other professionals, who may be able to assist you with your next move. Begin volunteering now, so when the time comes and you need someone to refer you, you have already put in the work to receive the promotion you deserve.

The best advice you'll ever get is this simple. Love your work so much, you are willing to do it for free.

A young man I know, an avid fan of B.B. King, happened to attend a university just down the road from a dedicated B.B. King museum. Every school year, that was the place you could find him in his every free moment - hanging out at the B.B. King museum, learning more about his hero. After visiting, reading, and talking to the staff for one full month, one of the staff members asked him if he knew someone who would be interested in volunteering in the Finance Department, assisting with filing and paperwork.

Coincidentally (or maybe not!), this student majored in Business Administration and knew enough about finance to assist with the tasks under the direction of the Finance Manager. After volunteering 10 hours a week for two months, he was thrilled to be invited to work a blues festival, where he met board members who governed the B.B. King museum. Because of his exemplary work and willingness to help out, the finance manager raved on their experience with him volunteering his time in their department, and as a result, the fan-turned-volunteer got a call the following Monday morning asking him to accept a full-time internship position working for the Finance department making $15 an hour.

He followed that golden rule through to its end. Love your work so much, you are willing to do it for free... at first!

He didn't interview for the internship position, nor did he apply to the position. I honestly don't think this position existed before he was willing to volunteer for free. People will make room for your gifts when you are willing to give your gifts for free!

Soul artist Betty Wright once sang, "in order to get something, you have to give something. In order to be something, you must go through something." I find volunteering to be a great opportunity to give your time and develop the crucial relationships that will move your career forward. Just like this young man experienced.

That said, not just any volunteer opportunity is a good one. As you move forward, seek opportunities that allow you to showcase your talents, and be sure the opportunity allows you to utilize your greatest skill-set.

The story of the B.B King fanatic launched into a career in finance from a part-time volunteer position is the story of my husband's very first internship. It started with his love, led to an opportunity, and eventually resulted in the start of his career! Ha! You must accept opportunities that align with your ideal work of service.

Let's say your major is health sciences. It's empathetic and heart-warming to feed the homeless during the holidays as a volunteer opportunity, but it may open more doors for you to volunteer your time serving with the American Red Cross or your local Health Department, so you are serving at an organization or in a position that allows you to be around healthcare.

Similarly, another great way to network to your next level is getting to know people in your industry, and seeing how you can help move their current projects forward. This is just like volunteering, but the service work will not be directly tied to an organization or a name you can put on your resume. Getting access to the practical work and learning beyond the textbook is ideal for all professionals. Many times this exposure requires you to be on the job and experiencing the work as it comes forward. Working with a professional in the industry will provide you with an opportunity to learn more about the current problems

THE NOT SO BUTTONED-UP APPROACH

at hand in a realistic way. You will have to choose wisely, though. Be sure this professional has a creditable history of helping others.

If you were asking yourself, "Where would I find these people?" The answer is vast and varied. You may find these people by talking to them at those big networking events, or you may see what they are doing in a local business magazine. You may hear about them from a friend or family member, or you might even find them on Instagram or LinkedIn. Whoever they are, or however you heard about them, your next step will be to contact that person directly and talk about your willingness to assist them with their work. People love to have help, but keep in mind that busy professionals are usually on the go. Do a little research, attend the next big event they are expected to be at, and interact with them there.

Here is how you should consider networking with professionals.

Before attending the event with a possible new connection, you must conduct your research and learn as much as you possibly can about them and the project(s) they are working on. Find out who is already on their team, and perform a gap analysis on the project to see who is missing. Then, figure out how your skills can help fill this void. This is how you will build value in yourself and your skill-set, and your affluent professional will have a lot harder time turning you down!

Once you have identified where your skills are needed the most, consider how you'll deliver your findings to the professional. You can't just walk up to them at the event and say, "I have identified a problem in your project." You have to get to know them first, talk about the project, and then speak on your 'value proposition'. What is your 'value proposition'? Basically, it is a big and complicated phrase that essentially describes the strengths and skills that you can bring to his or her project. And most importantly, why they should choose you to help!

Now, you are aiming to work on this project just like other professionals are, and therefore you must be strategic with your approach. Focus on being genuine, because people can see right through you when you are not. At the core of all business deals are not your skills, your abilities, or what university you attended. **It's that the decision maker must like you.** I have seen plenty of people with full and relevant skill sets be turned away from opportunities because the decision maker just didn't "trust" them. And you won't click with everyone! So make the goal when attending big networking events, to engage in three or four meaningful conversations that you can follow-up on and continue to build the relationship.

Need more examples?

My colleague Tiffany was summoned to attend a large technology conference to learn more about a new system her company was getting ready to implement.

THE NOT SO BUTTONED-UP APPROACH

During the conference, there was a major networking event, and although she was tired from the hustle and bustle of the day, she decided to go ahead and attend the networking event for an hour. During the event, she and about four other professionals were discussing a different software - one that she just so happened to have plenty of experience with.

She started to talk about the dos and don'ts, the ups and the downs and the pros and cons. Things that were still fresh in her mind from the recent integration of this technology with her current company. Eventually, the group ended the conversation and went to another restaurant to enjoy a couple of drinks, where the topic turned to her passion for integrating technology to make processes easier for both the company end-users and the customer.

This one-hour networking event turned into five hours, and at the end of the night she exchanged business cards with the professionals and went back to her hotel. When she got back, and before she went to sleep, she went to put the business cards in her wallet, and to her surprise, all of the professionals she had spoken to were Senior Executive leaders of large and prominent organizations. That next morning, she woke up to a phone call from one of them asking her to meet him for breakfast, where he presented her with an opportunity to work with their company, integrating the system she spoke so passionately about. As flabbergasted as she was, the executive went on to ask about her salary requirements, and when she would be available to get started.

No application, no interview, no cold calling, no checking of references. Five hours of connecting, filled with authentic conversation, landed her an opportunity to move up from an Assistant Project Manager to Project Manager at a much larger and more prestigious organization. Tiffany didn't know anyone beforehand, all she knew was the ins and outs of a system - her own, lived experience. But, since she knew the system inside out and outside in, someone wanted her expertise and knowledge. Ultimately, she networked for five hours to get an opportunity that wasn't even posted!

It took my husband a couple of months to land an opportunity. It took my colleague a couple of hours and who knows how long it will take you to network your way to success. As I mentioned in Chapter 1, there is no certain *time* to do anything... but be sure you are setting yourself up for success by indulging yourself in daily study of your industry and talking to industry leaders about current trends and issues.

So far, I've recommended that you volunteer your time and reach out to affluent professionals in your current industry. But what about learning more about your industry as a whole?

Joining organizations and associations is another great technique to network to the next level. While in college, you may have been asked or have joined your amazing alumni group, a fraternity, a sorority, or social

THE NOT SO BUTTONED-UP APPROACH

organizations. It is now time to use those associations to your advantage. While the most important reason to join an organization is to work to uphold the mission and carry out the cause, the second most important thing you gain from an organization is the ability to ask them for help when you need it.

Consider this. Since you have joined and worked very hard in the organization, you will have members who have seen your drive, compassion, personality and ability to handle tasks. These people would be more than happy to recommend you for the ideal job opportunity.

However, the truth of the matter is you must ask them to. Job opportunities go unfilled because most professionals in your associations do not know your major, interests, or ambitions. Don't just sit around and assume someone will consider you when a job opportunity opens. Be sure they know you would be interested. Politely inform decision makers in your association of your current career goals. Get ahead of them, and check out opportunities and departments in their company. Make time to talk about your desire to work there. I recommend that you do this casually, and make sure the conversation is suitable to have at the time you bring it up.

I tell you this as a cautionary tale. Don't join an organization and immediately ask someone to help you find a job. You must put in some work for others to be able to see your work. After you have made an effort, others will be willing to share your skills with their network. It is really that simple. This is how most professionals tap into what we call the "hidden market".

The hidden market is nothing but a secretive means of networking your way to success. It is a community of resources and information that never makes it to the public eye. These opportunities are protected and whispered about at networking events and to decision makers who can refer someone they can trust to the opportunity. The hidden market has existed since the beginning of time, and still does, despite many laws and legalities making it more difficult to operate using it.

However, more than half of fantastic opportunities will be found within the hidden market. This undisclosed group is the word-of-mouth connection where you must know someone that knows something about your skills and would be willing to recommend you for a job.

You know the saying, birds of a feather flock together. And it's true.

Movers and shakers typically associate themselves with similar people. College students usually hang with college students. Smart people usually hang with smart people and the hidden market is formed by these ecosystems genuinely seeking great talent.

Think of it this way, if a person generally surrounds themselves with smart people and a new position opens in their company, they are more likely to refer a friend they believe is also smart.

If you think this is unfair, you probably should work on improving your networking skills. You and I can both agree, it is hard to trust someone you don't know. You're certainly not going to put your own reputation on the line for someone you don't know, and neither would the person who would recommend you for your next awesome job.

Again, it's dating at its finest.

Imagine meeting a young professional at a networking event and after talking for about thirty minutes you find out he/she has your same major, attended the same school you attended, during the same time you attended school, and you don't know them. This would be strange to you, due to how unlikely a situation. Now, imagine them telling you they transferred during the same time you were gone for a semester on a co-operative assignment. You would be more likely to understand and halfway believe the professional if there was a way for you not to have met.

The way you would probably feel about this new professional who attended your school with your major is exactly how hiring managers, who are extremely involved in their industry, would feel. Who sent you? Why does no one know who you are? This is the very important reason why you must network. You must volunteer. You must get involved. And you must share your story with others so that they can make the connection to the next level.

As you begin to build these relationships and connect with professionals in your industry, please do not forget to say "Thank You" and to show you are actually thankful. This is a cardinal rule, and if you forget to be thankful and show your gratitude, your chances of getting to the next level will be slim. There is nothing more disappointing to a professional then to help someone and they are not thanked or informed about your opportunities. No one is going to ask you to thank him or her after they have assisted you, but you must remember to thank them. Saying thank you should be the quickest response you have after any interaction with a professional who has found interest in assisting you.

After someone answers your cold email from LinkedIn, be sure to send a thank you email. After someone accepts your request to go out for breakfast, lunch or dinner, be sure to prepare to pay for his or her meal. This is standard etiquette, if you ask someone to sacrifice their time to spend it with you, be sure it is worth their effort.

Now, I must admit, most high-level professionals will probably pay for your meal, but you must attempt and prepare to pay for the meal. It is common courtesy and it also shows professionalism. No matter what happens after breakfast, be sure to follow up with a hand-written thank you card with a nice surprise.

THE NOT SO BUTTONED-UP APPROACH

After someone spends more than 30 minutes of their time providing you with advice, feedback, resume review, goes out of their way to assist you, thank them. Acts of gratitude always seals the deal to any new relationship and just saying thank you is not enough.

Now that you have a full understanding of how to network to the next level, it is time for you to do so.

Here's how to get started.

Make a list of all the people in your life you are currently extremely close with who are professionals. This list will be people in your immediate family, your church, faculty members, your organizations etc. Please note, they must be extremely close to you. They must be someone you can call right now and ask for a favor.

Once you create this list, find out their career and their place of work. You may be able to do this by simply asking them or scrolling on LinkedIn to answer this question. Once you have found out where they work, conduct research on each of your immediate family members and get to know them professionally. How long have they been in their positions? What is their industry? Are they extremely active on LinkedIn? Do you feel comfortable enough to ask them for a favor?

Once you have put together this comprehensive list of immediate family, friends, faculty and community members, consider this to be your network. Start working your own network first, before reaching out to someone you don't know. This will give you the practice and the confidence you need to network with professionals outside of your network.

Now that you have your list together, it is time to "date" them. Say it with me again. Networking to the next level is dating at its finest.

Send a nice email, text message, or pick up the phone and professionally ask each person in your network for an opportunity to discuss your career development with him or her. Instead of going directly for a breakfast, lunch or dinner date, opt to have a 10-minute phone call to discuss your career goals. Since these people are already in your network, they will probably schedule a conversation with you easily. Your "built-in" network will probably be the easiest opportunity you will find to meet and talk with someone about your career without a chase. Everybody else, you will have to prepare to chase.

Before you share this phone call, be sure to prepare 5-7 questions for each of them. Great questions to get the conversation started are below.

- 1. How did you get started in your career?
- 2. Would you be willing to take me to a networking event with you and introduce me to some professionals in your network?
- 3. Do you personally know anyone who is searching for an entry-level grade in my field?

- 4. What associations or organizations do you recommend for me to join to connect with more professionals in my field?
- 5. What non-profit organizations do you heavily volunteer for? Are there any opportunities for me to attend an event and volunteer with you?

These questions will assist you in finding out exactly what you need to do to move forward. Each of these questions will give you action, and you need action. Once your contacts have provided you with answers to your questions, decide what networking events you would like to attend, what organizations you will be interested in volunteering with and you will also know what associations you should become involved in. Now the ball is back in your court, ready for you to take action. Don't forget to thank everyone who helped you as you begin to network to the next level.

Networking to the Next Level will take time, as I have mentioned to you before, but the goal is for you to truly display passion, commitment and your genuine interest in your career and advancing your industry. When you do this, your new career opportunity will land in your lap when you least expect it.

Question & Answer

Make a list of all the people in your life you are currently extremely close with who are professionals. This list will be people in your immediate family, your church, faculty members, your organizations etc. Please note, they must be extremely close to you. They must be someone you can call right now and ask for a favor.

Question & Answer

Find out and list each of these people's career and their place of work. How long have they been in their positions? What is their industry? Are they extremely active on LinkedIn? Do you feel comfortable enough to ask them for a favor?

Send a nice email, text message, or pick up the phone and professionally ask each person in your network for an opportunity to discuss your career development with him or her. Instead of going directly for a breakfast, lunch or dinner date, opt to have a 10-minute phone call to discuss your career goals. Record your notes in the space below.

Notes:

6

THE STORY THAT GETS HIRED

I recently received an email from an applicant who came across my advertisement for a social media intern. The email read:

DEAR MRS. HARRIS,
  Your search for a Social Media Intern just ended. I have attached my career portfolio for your review. Thank you for taking the time to read my information and I look forward to discussing this opportunity further.
  Respectfully,
  Taylor Jones

STARTLED AND COMPLETELY EXCITED TO OPEN THESE attachments, I stopped what I was doing and opened his career portfolio. To my surprise, it was the portfolio I had been looking for. Six pages of information that spoke exactly to my needs. It was creative, concise, factual (with data to back up his experience), and attached was an amazing reference list. I immediately picked up my phone and requested an interview with this student. His career portfolio was what I call, the "Chosen Portfolio".

A "Chosen Portfolio" is a collection of information about you that includes a well-written resume, a creative cover letter, a solid list of references, and a recent project list/case study.

When you are networking with high-level professionals,
When you are applying for job opportunities,
When you are applying for volunteer opportunities,
When you are applying for graduate school,
When you want to do anything major in life... opportunities will require you to present an outstanding career portfolio that talks about who you are, what you have already done to impact the world, your ability to work with diverse populations, and your unique goals.

Therefore, it is important for you to begin now to work on your "Chosen Portfolio".

This chapter will walk you through how to begin to create a "Chosen Portfolio" that is so thoughtfully curated that employers would want to speak with you now!

I decided to get into Career Development when I realized one of my greatest strengths was storytelling. However, like most people, my first resume looked like crap. It was bad. I mean crazy fonts, ugly formatting, too many pages bad.

But the one thing my resume had that many lacked was a compelling story. Part of my story is that I am the first person in my family to graduate from college. Yours might be something different. Start your resume with a 2-3 sentence summary of your story.

I was lucky enough that my compelling story landed me the opportunity to serve as the only work-study student for the Vice President of Admissions at my Junior College. My compelling story landed me the opportunity to interview to become a principal's secretary. The job was managing all registration for kindergartners, substitute teacher training, and the school-wide truancy report. I was 20 years old! Recently graduated from my 2-year (community college experience), attending my first semester at a four-year institution and I was the right-hand woman to the most important and well respected administrator at a K-2 grade school.

Let me backtrack a little and tell you how it happened. I had just finished my work-study program for the Vice President of Admissions, and I caught word that a position was opening up in the principal's office by a parent at a daycare center I was working at. She said the position was newly available, but they had someone in mind for the role already. That did not discourage me! I really thought I would be perfect for the job, so I went home, reviewed the job description and got to work as the position closed that same night.

THE NOT SO BUTTONED-UP APPROACH

Excited, yet anxious about the deadline, I completed the application.

But I was not done yet! I stayed up an extra two hours working on what I was going to do to get in front of the principal the following day.

When I awoke the next day, I immediately reached out to the principal by phone, but could not get hold of her. I then called the current secretary to see if I could get put onto Principal Thomas's calendar. The secretary drilled me so hard she scared me! I decided I had to take on a different approach. But first, one more call! After hanging up with the secretary, I called the central office and asked what times of the day the principal was usually in her office or available. She said, "You can sometimes catch her in the afternoon around 5."

That was all I needed to know. I went to the school around 4:45 p.m. got out of the car, went to the front desk, and asked to see the principal. The school looked closed for the day. No one was there but after school programs. The secretary I called earlier was out, and to my surprise, the lady at the front desk *was* the principal.

I smiled and took a deep breath. I told her exactly why I was there… and she invited me back! The moment she invited me to her office was the moment I knew I had a chance to land the position.

We talked in her office, and we talked seriously. I did not know how to use the computer systems they used, nor did I have firsthand experience in their record-keeping protocol. But I knew I had transferable skills. I was certain, I was going to get that job!

After speaking with Principal Thomas for thirty or so minutes she said, "Chandria, I haven't conducted interviews for the position yet. To be honest with you, I have someone who works internally that I had in mind for this position, but I want to give you a chance."

My foot was in the door!

She then went on, "I need someone who can start very soon, so they can be trained by our current secretary."

I smiled. "I can start tomorrow."

The next day I went to work (unofficially) as I watched the older, seasoned, more mature professionals walk into a room to interview with Principal Thomas, all while I was already training for the position! I literally got hired on the spot at 20 years old! While hiring policies and protocol have changed since then, my efforts and hustle can still be applied today. But even with your efforts and hustle, you can't come in empty-handed. So now, we go on to the "Chosen Portfolio".

Compelling Story

The "Chosen Portfolio" is more than just a resume, cover letter and list of references. When it comes to creating a "Chosen Portfolio", the first thing you must work on is crafting your compelling story. This story will share with readers your challenges, your lack of resources, and your ability to triumph through adversity. Your story will also talk about your accomplishments, organizations and charities you are involved in, and most importantly, how all these things have prepared you to become the person you are today... The person they want to hire!

Sit down and brainstorm what makes you unique. Once you have crafted your compelling story, write down the skills you have gained from your experiences, situations, and circumstances.

As a first-generation college graduate, I learned very early on how to speak for what I wanted and myself. I became the perfect negotiator. When something wasn't happening the way I thought was fair to all parties, I spoke up. One of my biggest strengths is communication. I often had to advocate for my family, and as a result I am good at articulating what people, not just myself, want. Believe it or not, I learned that unique skill at an early age!

Try and think of at least four strengths you have, things like communication, public speaking, mathematically inclined, critical thinking skills, problem solving, organization, etc. These are a part of your compelling story, and your compelling story is the foundation to a great resume. Now, it's time to begin writing!

. . .

THE WELL-WRITTEN RESUME

There is *no such thing* as a one-size fits all resume. Composing just one resume and sending it out to all employers is a No-No! It is the quickest way for you to receive that automated rejection at 10:00 p.m. when you know for a fact no one is in the office. Most companies use Applicant Tracking Systems that schemes through resumes for certain keywords to help recruiters. When a resume lacks a certain percentage of keywords, it loses rankings.

You might also have the question: What is the difference between a resume and a curriculum vita (CV)? Let's break it down.

A curriculum vita is an exhaustive list of everything you have ever done in life. A CV is like your career library. From jobs as a teenager, classes you have taken, presentations, published work, anything you have done in life: A CV is where you would house all of this information on your career.

A resume is a professional document crafted to respond to a request for employment and the needs of the opportunity you are applying to. Notice that I said "respond to a request". You will look at your curriculum vitae, taking the items that are applicable to this position, and respond to the job posting by crafting a resume for that specific opportunity. It should take the average job seeker about 4 hours to apply for one job opportunity, and this step will take up most of that time. Review the job description, and you will craft a response that will speak to the initial posting.

Now, let's address some rumors. Oftentimes, people will claim that certain parts of the resume are irrelevant or outdated. However, I am here to say that all resumes should include the following items: your contact information, a professional summary, your education, your skills, your accomplishments, recent work history, and civic engagements.

Let's break down these important sections.

Contact information:

I have reviewed over 1000+ resumes and so many of those resumes have left out important information such as their name and how to reach them. No matter how great your compelling story may be, if they don't know your name or your telephone number, how will they reach out to you? Always, always, double-check your contact information. It is totally okay for you to reveal just your city/state. Lose the entire address. Most companies don't send communication to your physical mailing address anymore, so this information can be removed if you wish. Be sure to add professional electronic portfolios such as your LinkedIn profile, your professional websites, and your online resume for review.

. . .

PROFESSIONAL SUMMARY:

The professional summary is the section of your resume where you get to share your compelling story. This section is often known as an objective. To be frank, an objective statement is totally self-centered. Unlike your cover letter, it doesn't really share with an employer what you can do for them. This is the place where you share how you can add value to their company. A great professional summary tells your compelling story, and adds your desires to the end. In the appendix, you will find an example of a great professional summary.

SKILLS/ACCOMPLISHMENTS:

This is the section of your resume where you will further explain the skills you have acquired that have gotten you to where you are today. Your resume will be competing in a global workforce. Be sure to show how you level-up to any other professionals by using data, numbers, facts, and information to prove that you are great! If you were in the Top 4 of your class out of 10,000 students, share that! You want employers to know you are worth every coin you will be asking for. (More on that later!) But as you notate your skills and accomplishments, be sure to state facts. Your future employers need to know exactly how you have competed in the past, and how that adds value to their organization.

Recent Work History:

Your recent work requires you to think outside the box. You know better than HR what your previous job entailed. Think outside of that job description! Your work history should state not only your title, but also the things you did both inside and out of your job description, exactly what you accomplished, and how you impacted your team. A great question to ask yourself is "How did you do something to save the supervisor?" It should share things that could have not been done if you weren't there. For an example: As an Internship Coordinator for a University, I increased internship placement by 50% within 2 years of employment.

The ultimate goal of a resume is to not only show that you meet the requirements and will be able to fulfill the job description, it is to show a future employer what you can do to help solve their current issues. When you look at a job description, view it as a problem someone needs to solve. Be sure everything you share on your resume addresses most, if not all, of these issues. It is okay for you to apply to opportunities where you don't meet all of the preferred requirements. However, to be realistic, be sure that you meet at least 75% of the requirements.

KEY WORDS:

The trick to writing a hirable, well-written resume is as simple as beating the applicant tracking system. The applicant tracking system (ATS) is a people management system that many companies use to rank resumes according to the qualifications requested by the hiring manager. With the right keywords, your resume could be ranked at the top of the pile.

Key words are specific words and phrases that describe the preferred skills, requirements, and qualifications that the hiring manager finds important. Remember when I mentioned that it is important to read and reread the job description, and tailor your resume language to address said job description? This is why.

When reading the job description, you will often notice certain words are used throughout the document. In particular, the "required skills", or "job requirements" section, will reveal all of the key words for you. When I am looking for keywords in my industry, I usually compare and contrast 3-4 job descriptions and identify words that are commonly used in each of them. This is my way of finding out exactly what words are considered important for that position. However, as tempting as it is, it is critical that you refrain from copying the job description word for word.

The applicant tracking system will highlight words and phrases that look exactly like the job description, and your resume will be flagged if your information directly copies what the job description states.

Be authentic, yet inspired. Look for the keywords, and creatively compose statements that truly describe your work. Remember: After the application comes the interview... and you don't want to get caught up in lies or reveal that you embellished your truth/skills!

STRUCTURE/FORMATTING:

For 99% of positions, basic resume formats filled with data and solid information, really are the best resumes. Most companies prefer very conservative resume formats with 12-point font size (at most), no crazy fonts (stick to the classic fonts: Times New Roman, Arial, Calibri), minimal pictures and graphics. However, if you are in a creative industry, this is totally different. It is hard to tell someone you are creative without the resume to prove it. It needs to show your skills on a resume.

For example, when I posted for a social media intern, the person who caught my eye most had a resume that was creative and concise. However, since the job posting requested someone who would be able to write creative content and create flyers, his resume was the perfect opportunity to share that information by showing me his creative side. His resume was the perfect mixture of creativity and cold, hard, facts. The creative arts industry usually welcomes fun, creative and entertaining resumes. But please remember, the hiring manager will still be looking for facts, data and accomplishments to prove your experience.

The Creative Cover Letter

Now, you've completed part one. But as I mentioned before, the "Chosen Portfolio" is a collection of resources and information about you that includes a well-written resume, a creative cover letter, solid list of references, and a recent project list/case study.

After writing the well written resume, it is now time to draft the creative cover letter. I suggest doing it in this order for this reason. Your cover letter will act as a synopsis of what your resume will display, and it is very challenging to write a creative cover letter before having a completed well-written resume.

The key questions you should consider when writing a creative cover letter are:

1. What problems did the job description state?
2. What experience do I have that solves them?
3. How can I begin to tell my compelling story that will welcome readers with enthusiasm?

When writing a creative cover letter, begin with a warm and innovative opening. Provide a recent accomplishment that will excite the reader and persuade them to continue reading. When the social media intern sent his career portfolio, I was blown

THE NOT SO BUTTONED-UP APPROACH

away by the first sentence in his cover letter. "The art to social media is to give the followers what they want in a way that will drive them to action." He even went further to say, "Over the last 2 years of college, I have created winning content and flyers that have placed the SGA Queen and President in their rightful positions. I would like to request candidacy for your Social Media Intern. My experience exceeds the preferred qualifications you are seeking." Spoken like a true campaign manager.

What his cover letter offered me was complete confidence, awareness and understanding of my needs. Every creative cover letter should offer the reader complete confidence in your understanding and awareness of the hiring manager needs. He was succinct, direct, and self-assured.

Yes, I said a cover letter should be succinct, so let's go line by line.

1. The first paragraph should be short and offer the reader a warm welcome that compels them to read further. Be polite and request candidacy, which means you are formally requesting an interview.

2. The second paragraph (4-5 sentences) should further speak to the needs discussed in the job description. Prove how you have solved those problems before.

3. The last paragraph should encourage the reader

to review more information on your resume and thank them in advance for the opportunity to interview with the company.

It is important to keep the cover letter one page and full of exciting yet factual content that will keep the reader involved. Below is the letter I received from our social media intern applicant, and eventual hire!

DEAR MRS. HARRIS,

The art of social media is to give the followers what they want in a way that drives them to action. Over the last 2 years of college at Mississippi University for Women, I have created winning content and flyers that have placed the Student Government Association Queen and President in their rightful positions. Not only did I listen to the vision of my clients, but I also portrayed this information to the audience, ultimately allowing them to serve in their current roles. I would like to request candidacy for the Social Media Intern position. My experience exceeds the preferred qualifications you are seeking and I am confident I will help you move your business forward.

Social media is my thing. I am a Digital Marketing Junior with a 3.4 GPA. From using Canva, Adobe, and Keynote, to starting from scratch on Microsoft Word, I am very proficient in all of these systems and use them to create content for class and student organizations on campus. I am absolutely in love with strategizing and brainstorming on best sayings, hashtags, weekly insights, and analytics that business owners like you need to know.

I am able to not only create content but also post the information for you: which will give you a complete peace of mind to handle other things. My resume will further display how I am working my magic each day. I am very confident you will find my skills to be everything you need. I welcome the opportunity to interview with you at your convenience.

Thank you for reading my email.

Kind regards,

Sadie

THIS COVER LETTER example is one of the many ways you can capture the Hiring Manager's attention. But first you need to outline your compelling story, know what the client needs, and clearly articulate how you can solve their problems.

THE CASE STUDY:

AFTER THE CREATIVE cover letter and the well-written resume comes a badass case study! I am crazy in love with this section of your "Chosen Portfolio".

A case-study project list is a summary of three

recent projects you have worked on, and your view on how you impacted the project. It is perfect for job seekers across all industries to be able to further explain and display their impact on an organization or company. When writing your case-study project list, be sure to only include stories that will further drive home your ability to do the job at ease. Again, I am using our social media intern applicant to showcase his use of the case study in his "Chosen Portfolio".

Project: Sadie runs for President of Mississippi University for Women, Student Government Association

My Tasks: Creating social media content, graphics, and infographics to give to solicit and engage followers, faculty and community.

Implementation Time: We started this project two months before the actual campaign. Sadie initially hired me to help her create her message and her theme. I came up with the colors, slogan, hashtags, graphics and social media content. She gave me full liberty to design her vision (see attachment).

Results: Sadie's social media followers increased by 45% within two months of working with her. She also won the Presidential race!

. . .

THE NOT SO BUTTONED-UP APPROACH

YOUR ULTIMATE GOAL is to show a future employer how you will impact their company. You need data. You need facts. You must tell your compelling story!

LIST OF REFERENCES:

Now if you didn't already guess, Sadie made his list of solid references. He included four other professionals. Two professors, the reigning SGA Queen (a previous client), and his academic advisor. He truly provided me with everything I needed to know to make a sound judgment about his ability to help me.

When you are creating your solid reference list, be sure to tell your reference you have put them down and outline what you have put them down for. I also recommend that you list an email as well as a telephone number, along with a project/task this person could talk with the hiring manager about.

Example: Tiffany Jennings – Professor (Mississippi University for Women) Known for 2+ Years | Ms. Jennings will be able to further speak with you about my character, grades and ambition. Contact Tjennings.24@aol.com | (234) 892-3212

FINISH YOUR BUSINESS:

Once you have completed your career portfolio, be sure to have some take a look at your information. You want your "Chosen Portfolio" to be free of grammatical errors and typos. Remember, it is important to tweak and make changes to your career portfolio when applying to each job opportunity. Your goal is to let the employer know that you created this information just for them.

CHOSEN PORTFOLIO

Use the space below to draft your "Chosen Portfolio." What skills and references would you include? What would you include in your professional summary?

SKILLS

REFERENCES

SUMMARY

7

LANDING THE DREAM CAREER

The process leading up to you landing the job of your dreams comes with a lot of commitment. You must be committed to finding the perfect job, showcasing why you are the perfect candidate for said job, winning professionals over so that you can be placed in that job, and ultimately landing the job! Of all the phases of the job-search process, interviewing is by far my favorite part. I have always told my friends and family, "If I could just get the interview, I know I will get the job!"

In this chapter, I will be sharing with you the techniques that have landed students and young professionals their interviews and job opportunities with world-famous Fortune 500 companies with top-notch salaries to match their badassery!

. . .

"Mrs. Harris,

Thank you for coming in today. You have an amazing resume and we absolutely love what we have heard so far. Come on back!"

Dressed to impress in my grey tailored suit skirt, 3-inch navy closed toe pumps, and a crisp white blouse, I stood up and proceeded to walk into the interview of my dreams! As I walked to the room I began to think about everything I have ever done that has prepared me to be in this place today.

I said a silent prayer, thanked my ancestors, and as the knob turned on the door to the conference room I told myself, "You are going to kill this interview."

In the interview room, I noticed five diverse smiling faces. Two men, three women. Three seasoned leaders, two young professionals, and an open seat for me! I took my seat, opened my portfolio, smiled at the hiring committee, and was ready to go to work.

To start the interview, one of the young professionals thanked me again for coming in to the interview. He followed his thanks with my favorite question of all time, "Tell me about yourself."

Boy, did I tell him! They each followed up with more questions, and after each one was asked, I felt more empowered to showcase my accomplishments. Everything in my heart told me I did exceptionally well as I answered my final questions, shook their hands, and marched to the car like I was the CEO! Not thirty minutes went by and your girl was hit with a phone call and an offer... and at that moment, I knew I had interviewed like one too!

I landed the job of my dreams and you can do it too when you commit to fully understanding the company, sharpening your interview skills, and mentally preparing to blow the hiring committees away!

The first step to landing any career opportunity is gathering a great sense of understanding and knowledge about the company. This is by far the longest step in your interview preparation phase, but if you take the time to prepare properly, you will outshine most of your competition. To get a better understanding on how to properly prepare for the company, you have to not only talk like the CEO in an interview, but first and foremost study the company like you are interviewing for a CEO position.

The moment you get word you have landed an opportunity to interview with a particular company is the moment you must begin to study their product/services, their mission, their objectives, and how the department you seek to work with answers to the company's mission and objectives.

Studying the Products/Services

Every company has a customer/client base and a target audience. Studying the product, services, and offerings will allow you to learn exactly how the job you recently applied to serves the target audience. You must learn all you can about their services by working with the product/services.

Almost every company has a website with a YouTube video on their services and how they do things. From the music in the background, to the actors used to reveal their products and services, that promotional video will be a great resource for you to get a better understanding of their services and the way they deliver the services.

- Once you understand and have gathered a great sense of knowledge on their services and products, you will now need to find out how the department you could potentially work for actually fits in with the mission, objectives, and delivering the product or services. The questions you should ask yourself areHow does the department I want to work in impact the services this company offers?
- How can I add value to what they are looking for?

As a Career Consultant, I assist career services

departments and employers with recruiting and retaining young professionals. When I am interviewing for a business opportunity or an opportunity to speak with their students and services, I always check out what programs and events they have offered their students/employees recently and what can I do to further enhance their goals and mission. **Always, always, always get as close as possible to the product/services and offerings from a company when you are trying to get hired.** The interview conversations will be a breeze once you have had a chance to learn more about the services.

Another great way to understand more about the company and the department you would like to work for, is to follow their news and trends! At any given moment something good or bad could happen with a company that could provide opportunities to add more people to the team.

I have a client who recently reached out to me because he was watching the morning news and found out a large company was coming to an area. He was a business finance young professional, and thought this would be a great chance to get in good with the company early. He began to study why the company was moving, dove deep into studying the product and services, and followed his studies by reaching out to a recruiter on LinkedIn about positions.

The recruiter was extremely excited about speaking with him because he knew there would be lots of positions open and the recruiter already had a talented candidate inquire. It was a great moment for the recruiter to start recruiting. One thing led to the next, he got the interview and was one of the earliest hires in town.

If a new company moves into town, we would automatically assume they would be flying current employees in to work. But we would also automatically assume they would need employees who are currently living in the area to assist with turnover from the move and truly understand the new market. Knowing how long the company has been in an area and knowing where the company is headquartered, will also provide you with more insight about the company, and will give you an opportunity to leverage your experience in the town/city over other competition.

THE NEXT BIG step in the preparation process is to learn more about their strategic plan, mission, and objectives. This information will tell you more about what direction the company is heading and why they are going in that direction. Researching the company's stock, financial report (if it's available), their strategic initiatives, and things they would like to accomplish will allow you to find exactly where you fit in. It will allow you to see how your current skill set will empower and add value to their team.

One of my higher education friends who works

with grants and contracts identified a great position by going to the official grant website to see what nonprofits and organizations were recently awarded funds from the federal government. When a company comes into new money, there is a big chance they may be hiring new people. The companies in her area who received the most, also received a nice email and follow-up call from her. Within a month, she was hired on a new grant contract to help a nonprofit!

Understanding the mission, structure, products and services of a company will help boost your confidence and speak intellectually about the company. Nothing excites hiring committees more than a knowledgeable candidate.

Once you have a thorough understanding of the company products and services, it's time to sharpen your interviews skills!

S*harpening* Interview Skills

All over the internet you will find common interview questions, methods to interview properly and examples for you to truly ace your interview. Since this information is all over the web, recruiters and hiring committees will expect you to know what to say and how to say it. But to be honest with you, following methods of interviewing sometimes works in your favor, but the most important thing you must be able to do in an interview is to show the hiring committee exactly how you will add value and help with their current tasks. Being knowledgeable about the company, knowledgeable about your skills and being able to *prove* your experience is what you must do in any interview.

In my years of experience, I have found many hiring committees are trained to ask any of the 8 types of questions below.

1. Opinion questions (Scenario Questions)

The purpose of these types of questions is to examine how you would act and behave to certain situations.

2. Experience verification questions

This kind of question is geared toward finding out what type of problems you have solved and what analytical skills you gained in school to prepare you for their position. The purpose of this question is to evaluate experience in your background.

3. Credential verification questions

This kind of question helps HR people gauge hard facts such as what degree did you earn? What was your GPA? The purpose of this question is to gather hard evidence of your educational accolades.

4. Stress questions

These types of questions are sometimes used to throw you off of your pre-programmed answers and to see how you can think on the spot. These are no right or wrong answers. They really want to see how well you think on your feet.

5. Behavioral questions (Most common type of interview question)

This type of question wants you to explain yourself thoroughly and reveal to them how you will handle a situation or how you have handled a certain situation. This is the most commonly used interview type question.

6. Competency questions

This type of question is designed to measure your past behaviors and to see if they align with specific competencies required for the position. Hiring committees may ask questions such as, "Tell me how you would creatively solve a problem? Will you give me an example of how you have led teams in the past?"

7. Case questions (Large companies usually use these type of questions)

This type of question puts you to the test on the spot. They will measure your ability to problem solve, critically think, manage stress levels, and your methods to identifying solutions to problems.

8. Technical questions

These questions will measure your ability to use certain software, tools and programs. HR committees will test your calculation skills, ability to proficiently use programs and solve common day-to-day problems. Technical questions are used in every industry, and the form will vary!

With these 8 types of questions, most companies usually ask anywhere between 10-15 questions, depending on what they would like to know about you and how the conversation goes. I have heard of professionals getting hired after 30 minutes, I have heard of stories where professionals were in interviews for 2 hours and didn't get the position.

However, I have provided 10 common questions and a key for you to answer each of them!

1. Q: Tell me about yourself?

A: They want to know only about your education, career, and background that has led you to apply to this position.

2. Q: Why should we hire you?

A: They want you to highlight your values, impact, and show that you are fully equipped to answer to the responsibilities outlined in the job.

3. Q: What are your strengths?

A: They want you to discuss your strengths and how you will do your job well.

4. Q: What are your weaknesses?

A: They want you to bring out the human side and share a real weakness with actions you have taken to solve these issues. Be sure to not share a weakness that will be detrimental to the position. For instance, you shouldn't apply to a banker position and struggle with math!

5. Q: What do you know about the company?

A: This is when your research comes full circle. You

want to discuss what you know about the company, the positives and how you would like to add to their success!

6. Q: What have you done in the past to properly prepare for the role?

A: They want hard facts and for you to share stories on how you have experienced, completed, and were involved in certain tasks that sharpened your skills to be great at the job you have applied to.

7. Q: What are you looking for in a position?

A: Ideally, it should be the position you are interviewing for. Never quote the job description word-for-word but be sure to align what you look for with what they are offering.

8. Q: What type of animal would you be and why?

A: The fun stress question tests your ability to think on your feet. Be clever in your answer and be sure it matches the role you are interviewing for.

9. Q: Tell me about a time you weren't able to meet a deadline?

A: This is a conflict resolution question to see how you will solve problems. Provide a complete story of the issues and talk them through exactly how you positively answered the questions.

10. Q: Do you have any questions for us?

A: Always a yes! You want to ask questions about the department, the culture, your job requirements, their needs and when they would like for someone to start! This is the perfect time to interview *them* and to see if you are still interested in working for them!

THE MOST COMMON form used to answer questions is this method called the STAR Method! Almost every company in every industry has adopted the Star Method, which is great to use when answering any type of the 8 interview questions. STAR stands for:

Situation – Discuss a challenge/situation and tell the story?

Task – What was your area of responsibility? What were you required to do?

Action – What steps did you take to solve the problem? How did you handle the issue and why did you handle it that particular way?

Results – Good or bad, what happened, what did you learn from the issue?

When answering interview questions, you want to first tell the story and the situation. Then you want to follow up with your tasks. It's always nice to add in what your team has done but remember this is your interview, so you must sell the interviewers on how *you personally* handled a certain task.

The key to interviewing is to not only know how to answer the questions, but it is also knowing how to articulate each story you tell in a way that truly exposes your key skills and strengths. Painting the picture to be extremely clear with a lot of confidence and zero arrogance.

Once you have sharpened your skills, now you must mentally prepare for the actual interview. Whether the interview is via phone, in person, Skype or over dinner, each of these settings will force you to tell someone all about your strengths!

I don't know why we as humans struggle with sharing our story and skills, but it is common across the board. Most people cringe at telling someone how good they are at something.

Any interview is the perfect place for you to shout to the damn room why you are special. It is the perfect time to tell all interested parties about how you have made your way, through the ups and downs of school, through crazy bosses, amazing assignments, and gossipy coworkers. This is the time to focus solely on you, your skills, your education, your impact, your value, your badass-ness and you must be mentally prepared to do so.

Before the interview of my dreams, I said a nice prayer and I whispered to myself, "You are a badass and you will kill this interview." Any interview environment will be extremely stressful and somewhat tough! You may interview with one person, two people, a committee, the CEO, the hiring manager, the janitor. Hell, whomever they put in the room to talk to you, you must be prepared to do that. You must be able to look past all of their interview scare tactics and focus

THE NOT SO BUTTONED-UP APPROACH

on why you are there. The toughest battle in any interview room is the candidate's battle with themselves. Interviewers can definitely tell when you forgot to say something you wanted to say, they can tell if you don't have a clue, and they can definitely tell when they have gotten under your skin.

The trick to all of their interviewing techniques is to know who you are, understand why you were picked to interview, and they need someone just as bad as you want to work for them. At the end of the day, they need you. They found something in your skillset to convince them you would be perfect for the job. Don't ever forget that!

No matter how crazy they may get, how hot the room may be, or if one person never looks at you during the interview, these people need someone to come in quickly and take the load of work off of them. They are frustrated, performing two to three people's jobs, and they need someone to come in now. Consider their interviewing techniques as a cry for help, and **you are there to help them.**

Once you have mentally prepared to do well during the interview, you must prepare your questions to ask. Interviewing is a two-way street and you must have meaningful questions in order to truly gauge the environment, the roles, the expectations, the potential boss, and next steps in the interview process. You would want to get a full 3-D view on the opportunity so that you can make an informed decision by choosing to invest at least eight hours of your day with this company for at minimum two years. I highly advise all of my clients to ask at least 5 questions. Here are some common questions I think are extremely necessary to ask during any interview.

1. **Will you please share with me how this opportunity came about?** This is the perfect question to learn more about their retention, and the position.

2. **If you had to choose the number one skill needed to successfully perform the duties required for this role, what would your number one skill be?** This question forces the hiring manager and the team to tell you exactly what they are looking for. This is the perfect question to see where you are in the running. If the number one skill needed is something you are absolutely great at doing, this question will be confirmation. If the number one skill needed is something you have some but little experience in, then you will also know what skill you need to sharpen or prove you can do.

3. **Please walk-me through a typical day in the life of this position.** Please state the name of the position. This is a great question to see if they know the ins and outs of the role, and it is also great for you to measure job demands, stressors, challenges and strengths. If you apply to a position that will require you to sit at your desk for 5 hours of the day and you really like to move around a lot, this may be an issue!

4. I **am extremely interested in learning more**

THE NOT SO BUTTONED-UP APPROACH

about your management style. This question/statement will encourage the hiring manager to share with you how they oversee and govern their employees. Great question to learn all about how your manager will behave at work. This is important because if you hate micromanagers or need someone to provide you with specific details on how to do a role, they will probably reveal their management style during this time.

5. **If selected to move forward in the process, what should I look forward to?** This question will provide you with clarity on what is going to happen next. They will reveal if there are more interviews, when the position is expected to be filled, and how things will move forward after this meeting.

Asking great questions will prove to the hiring committee you are truly invested in their company and the opportunity. It is also the perfect time for you to watch behaviors, side-eyes, catch B.S., and ask yourself "Is this the place for me"? Just because it is an opportunity, it doesn't necessarily mean this is the one you must take. Follow your gut, not your heart! If your intuition is telling you this place is a mess, run as fast as you can out of the door!

Landing your dream career is all about committing to putting in the work to show your potential colleagues you are knowledgeable and equipped to come in and do the work. When you take the time to get to know the company, sharpen your interview skills, and mentally prepare for the interview, you will prove to any employer you are not only capable of carrying out the duties assigned for the position you have applied to, but you will also prove you are heavily invested in working for their company.

INTERVIEW EXERCISE

Tell me about yourself?

Why should a company hire you?

What are your strengths?

INTERVIEW EXERCISE

What are your weaknesses?

What are you looking for in a position?

Tell me about a time you weren't able to meet a deadline?

8

MUST-HAVE CRITICAL SKILLS

Over my tenure in Human Resources, I have had the opportunity to attend several different career conferences including NCDA (National Career Development Association) and NACE (National Association for College & Employers). The topic that comes up time and time again is the topic of *transferable skills*. Career professionals like me have talked to employers, our colleagues, and industry leaders, and the top three skills that we look for in young professions the most are the ability to Communicate, Critically Think, and Collaborate well with others. This shit is complicated, and young professionals are losing their jobs because they can't seem to get it right.

Communication
Having the technical skills and the degree is not

enough in today's job market. If you think about most career paths, you can pretty much be taught anything unless it is an industry specific opportunity such as lawyer, physician, chemist, or engineer. But let's be real, most undergraduate students are not graduating with these degrees. For all other opportunities, if someone likes you and your work ethic, the job can be taught to you. Transferable skills are the way to success.

There are many skills that prove important in your professional success, but hands down young professionals are dinged the most on communication. Recently, I attended a networking event and I had an opportunity to speak directly with a Vice President of a Fortune 500 company. Our conversation surprised me. I asked him for the issues he had noticed most when it came to dealing with young professionals, and he looked to me and said communication. He ranted for five minutes making claims like, "They are obsessed with their phones."

"I know technology is important but it doesn't trump communicating." His rant continued, "They walk around with headphones in their ears, never make eye contact and think that something is wrong with us."

Well, as you can see, this VP had a big issue with young professionals and I couldn't defend us. Sometimes we communicate very poorly - or worse, not at all.

At that same conference, I had another Vice President who shared a story that was funny to me, but awfully painful to him. He had recently hired an entry-level professional whose birthday was coming up. Although the employee didn't directly report to the Vice President, the VP wanted the guy to feel special with a personal birthday phone call.

Some VPs want to be seen as reachable. They will give you their personal cell number for important stuff and even have their Secretary reach out to them if a young professional calls. But this VP phoned the new hire, and the new hire didn't pick up the phone. The VP left a voicemail and asked the new hire to get in touch with him. After the VP hung up the phone, he immediately decided to call the employee's supervisor and ask if he was in that day. The Supervisor said yes, and that he must have stepped away from his desk.

The supervisor then went and found the employee and told him to check his voicemail. He told him that he might have a voice message he would like to hear. The new hire checked his voicemail and to his surprise, it was a Happy Birthday message from the Vice President of the company!

The new hire was extremely excited. He texted the VP, "Thank you for your birthday message." Pissed, the VP then phoned the Supervisor and asked him, "Does this new guy not know how to use the corporate phone correctly?"

He assumed the young professional didn't know

how to pick up the phone and return the call because of this new hire's grand idea to text the VP.

I tried to hold it in, but it was so funny I had to laugh. I asked him, "Did you really think the guy didn't know how to use the phone?"

As serious as he could be, he said, "Yes."

There are three main ways to communicate effectively as potential employers want you to:

1. By Speaking
2. By Listening
3. By Writing

#1. Speaking

You must know what to say, how to say it, and when to say it. Always think before speaking. Consider your environment, your audience, and your message. Be sure your message is crystal clear. Keeping all of these things in mind, it's crucial for you to practice your grammar, study linguistics, and be on point with your language, your diction and most of all, your manners.

I once had a student who came into my office and asked me, "What is my jurisdiction of duties today?" I was like huh? Jurisdiction? Cool word to use at the wrong time. Your words should be relevant to the conversation and the subject. Do not try and look smart by using words that don't make sense, or by using words you are not entirely sure of the meaning.

Be sure all parties listening can clearly understand exactly what you are saying.

#2. Listening

The best advice I ever received was to listen to understand, instead of listening to respond. I love small talk. It's so funny to me when I ask someone, "How are you today" and their answer is "You too." Huh? You did not listen at all. Great listeners take pride in repeating a word or a small phrase that was last spoken by the person before them. It tells the person you are communicating with that you are listening with opening ears. The same goes for the workplace. If your supervisor ever gives you an assignment verbally, be sure to write down everything.

#3. Writing

Clear written communication is your bread and butter. You must be able to write clearly and concisely with a subject, verbs, pronouns, and adjectives. The saddest thing about writing is most of us have learned standard English and writing for 12+ years of our life and we still seem to screw it up. There are so many books, articles, and resources out there for you to practice your skills. My favorite book on writing is called, *"Watch Your Words: A Writing and Editing Handbook for the Multimedia Age" by Marda Dunsky*. There is plenty of guidance, and exercises in the book that will truly help you with writing and grammar.

Communication is an extremely important skill and professionals who do it best are the ones who go far. Technical skills are important, but you'd be surprised how far you can go as an exceptional communicator.

CRITICAL THINKING

When someone mentions critical thinking, the first thing that usually pops up in your head is solving a difficult mathematics or science problem. You may even think about Taraji P. Henson in Hidden Figures and the long math equations she solved. But that is not what critical thinking really is.

Critical thinking is being able to think on your feet and make a sound judgment in a demanding or time sensitive situation.

I'm a data girl, and in most of my positions, I have housed all of the data.

Once I had a supervisor who requested numbers from me about career placement and he needed them by noon. The email that came across my desk was sent at 11:33 a.m. - less than half an hour before the deadline. He asked me to text him the answers as soon as I could. I stopped working on my current assignment and sent over to him the analysis of the career placement report. Yes, it was difficult and I was mad as hell that he was asking this from me so last minute, but for whatever reason he needed it now and I was going to do my best to get it to him. After the meeting he apologized for the time constraint and thanked me over and over for getting the work done without asking more questions.

Sometimes your supervisor may not be able to answer all the questions you have when an assignment is given under an extreme timeline. You are expected to really do your best without an attitude and without running around the office yelling about it. You're expected to think critically.

Most critical thinking situations will require you to do the following.

- IDENTIFY the situation or problem
  - Research what you can to fix it or solve it
  - Evaluate if you think the research or your findings are correct or suitable for the situation
  - Draw a conclusion based off your judgment
  - Decide what is important or relevant
  - Present the information as clearly as possible.

I KNOW an employee who was a wonderful secretary to one of our VPs. While it seems basic, she used her critical thinking skills in a great way during a potentially stressful time for her supervisor. This secretary reported to work one Tuesday morning, and looked at

THE NOT SO BUTTONED-UP APPROACH

her supervisor's calendar (as one does). That Tuesday, she noticed an impromptu lunch meeting.

When her supervisor walked into his office, he greeted his secretary and went straight to the conference room. Not long after, no less than ten people joined him. It was only 10 a.m. but she thought to herself, "Do they have lunch planned for this meeting?"

During the meeting, she texted her supervisor and said, "I am ordering lunch for the meeting attendees. Please confirm how many people are in the meeting."

Not long after he responded, "Ten. Thank You."

While she was the real hero, her supervisor was proudly able to declare that he had taken care of lunch. Not only did he get bragging rights for taking care of food during this impromptu meeting, but he also sang the employee's praises because of her initiative.

She did everything right. She read her supervisor and knew to take care of the knitty gritty details. What would they like to eat? What time would he like the food ordered? What type of drinks would people want? She took initiative and did not worry about the small details, as her supervisor had bigger fish to fry. She ordered something everybody could eat and drink, then had the food delivered immediately.

Being able to think critically is the type of transferable skill that will get you promoted quickly. When you think critically, you are able to have your boss's back during stressful situations!

. . .

Collaboration

Have you ever worked on a project or a team with someone whom it was extremely difficult to get information from? Unfortunately, it happens all the time in the workplace. Because most roles intersect in some way, shape, form, or fashion, you may get a colleague who refuses to be a team player.

Collaboration is a nice and fancy word that means being a team player. In every work environment, all employees are expected to be great team players, and that will require a great deal of collaboration.

I have a really good friend who is catching hell from her colleague. As the Sales and Marketing Coordinator at a very large hotel chain in the United States, she is responsible for ensuring all sales and catering events are successfully planned and executed. After the events are over, she has to report the event's guest count, food revenue, and other data to her supervisor. However, the person who oversees all of this data at the hotel doesn't like to pull a weekly report for my friend. Instead of nagging her supervisor to talk to the guy and get her reports, she decided to take matters into her own hands.

She scheduled a meeting with him to see what was up. To her surprise, she found out that he was extremely understaffed, and he didn't have the manpower to pull the report each week. Working in catering, she understood that first hand and asked if he would be willing to show her how to pull the report.

He taught her how, and now she pulls her own catering sales reports each week. Now, the two have a great relationship and are able to pull the data and numbers together!

In order to be considered a person who is great at collaboration, you must be good at managing expectations. Be open to new ideas and changes. And be someone who can help clarify the goals and objectives of a project.

Education and experience are the prerequisites to getting a career opportunity. Embodying solid transferrable skills is what lands you the career opportunity. You see, this stuff is complicated and trust me when I say, I didn't embody all of the skills when I graduated college. But that is okay! Your next step is to analyze what transferable skills you possess, and begin to work harder on the skills that are a challenge to you.

Career Development is a journey to a worthy destination and the journey begins with understanding of who you are, how you would like to impact the world, and the next step to strengthen your skills. This means you must embody the necessary resources, tools, and transferable skills to exceed what is expected of you.

Being the person who got fired because you didn't write professional emails is not cool.

Being the professional who didn't get the job because you didn't display your critical thinking skills in an interview is not cool.

Being the professional who is talked about amongst

senior leaders because you don't play well with other employees is also not cool.

And when you are not cool in the workplace, someone will happily escort you out the door.

I said all that to say, as an entry level professional, you must be able to clearly articulate your ideas in a way that empowers your colleagues to not only interact with you but also welcome your input. You must be able to meet the needs of the entire staff and critically think when they are in need of you the most. You must be intentional about your daily assignments and only present your best work to the staff. Only then will you have mastered all of the C's. I know it's complicated, but as time moves along, I have faith in your ability to get it right.

Find an opportunity to practice your critical thinking skills, following these steps:

Identify the situation or problem
Research what you can to fix it or solve it
Evaluate if you think the research or your findings are correct or suitable for the situation
Draw a conclusion based off your judgment
Decide what is important or relevant
Present the information as clearly as possible.

Record your experience (and the outcome!) below.

9

SHOW UP AND SHOW OUT

"We are what we repeatedly do. Excellence then, is not an act, but a habit." - Aristotle

"Your daily behavior reveals your deepest beliefs." – Robin Sharma

"Winning is a habit. Unfortunately, so is losing." – Vince Lombardi

"Good habits are the key to all success." - Og Mandino

"Success is the sum of small efforts repeated day in day out." - Robert Collier

"If you want to change your world, you need to start cultivating good habits."- Mina Tadros

"If your habits don't line up with your dream, then you need to either change your habits or change your dream." - John Maxwell

. . .

THE NOT SO BUTTONED-UP APPROACH

READ THE QUOTES ABOVE. Make sure you really read them. Do you get it? You must form habits. Not only that, but you must form good habits, or else you are in trouble. Habits run our lives and whether they are good habits or bad habits, we will be affected by the patterns and things we decide to do each day. I once read the book, *What the Most Successful People Do Before Breakfast: A Short Guide to Making Over Your Mornings—and Life* and I quickly begin to question two things.

#1. Did I truly want to be a successful person?

#2. If I have to get up at 5:00 a.m. in the morning every day to talk to executives, will they actually get a call from me?

In order to prepare yourself to be an exceptional employee or an exceptional executive you must begin to form great habits. College was your days of fun. You were able to make your own schedule, show up to class if you wanted to, make a fake copy of a doctor's note and turn it in to your favorite professor, and then go about your day. No one was going to check on you, you didn't have to answer to anyone but yourself, and life was great. You could even plan when you were going to skip class. If you were like me, you and I both formed horrible habits in college and I definitely paid for them when I entered the workplace.

I talk to several employers on a daily basis and there are a two dumb reasons why new employees get fired.

Not showing up to work at all.

Not showing up to work on time.

Yes, those college days are over and attendance and punctuality is extremely important in the workplace. I know a student who was hired to serve as a project manager for a Fortune 500 company making close to six figures right out of college. He was living the life. They moved him to a big city, gave him a company car, a large office, and he oversaw about four employees.

Well, after three months on the job, I received a call from the student asking if he could come by the office to visit with me. Of course I was happy to hear all about the exciting things he was doing, so I scheduled something for that day. When he stopped by, he looked very sad, puzzled, and down. I asked him what was wrong, and as you may have guessed, yes, he had been fired. The company he worked for managed their employees with a point system and any time you were late to work, you were given a certain amount of points. He reached enough points in those three months that his six-figure job opportunity ended, and out the door he went.

I highly recommend you strengthen four specific habits to build amazing business acumen and workplace rapport. These habits will make you look like a freaking executive compared to other entry-level professionals who don't have a clue.

Build the following habits, and you'll be considered a rockstar.

. . .

Habit #1: Show up & Show Out

To be on time is to be late and to be late is unacceptable. Time management is one skill you must strengthen. You really don't have a choice. Time is of the essence for everybody and it is one thing of those things in life we really cannot get back. When a time has been set for you to go to work, attend a meeting, take a call, complete a task, it is expected to be completed in a timely manner because the time that has been measured out to complete that task is structured with a ROI (Return of Investment) in mind. The time that has been agreed upon for you to arrive at work is the time that has to be paid for and when an employee doesn't report to work on time, he or she is ultimately wasting the company's money. Of course, punctuality is a part of your mutual agreement, and you must adhere to that.

When you show up, you must show out! Come dressed for success with a wardrobe that will make you feel comfortable and prideful to be where you are. Even if where you are is not where you would ultimately like to be, prepare for your future by creating a habit of dressing to impress. Since there is only one opportunity to make a great first impression, it is always important to dress as if you are ready to take a meeting, attend an impromptu lunch, or have a sit down with an executive at your company. Sometimes those opportunities are planned, but other times they are not.

A couple of months ago, I walked into the faculty dining room at the university where I work, hungry and tired. I really wanted to take my lunch back up to my office and eat alone. However, there were other plans for me. As I joined the long line, I heard one of my favorite colleagues yell, "Chandria, come sit with us!"

As you know, I really didn't feel like conversing during my lunch break but I glanced at the table and the President of the University was sitting there. I told myself I had no choice. I had to muster up some strength, poise, and genuine excitement, and join a table full of executive staff. As I was pulling out my chair to sit down, the President said to me, "Chandria, your dress looks really nice."

I thought to myself, "I didn't think I was having lunch with my President this morning when I put my clothes, but boy, I am glad I usually show-up and show out at work!"

When you show-up and show out, and it is not something you only do when you are happy or when someone asks you to wear a certain outfit, you have a reputation that is subconsciously being formed in the minds of others. As superficial as it seems to some, they will automatically assume you are intelligent, business savvy, and hardworking.

I'm not saying all professionals truly embody those

great adjectives, but they usually get the reputation to start with, simply because of the way they dress. Therefore, wherever you decide to go, to a networking event, work, dinner, or volunteer, be sure you are dressed in your best and you would be comfortable having a conversation with prestigious professionals. I'm not going to tell you what to wear or how to wear it, however your clothes must be suitable for the situation and should always make you feel confident.

When professionals show up to work five to ten minutes before their shift begins, it allows them time to mentally prepare for the day. They are not rushing to work full of anxiety and hoping no one is there or talking about them. Get to work on time, dress to impress and prepare to leave five minutes after your shift is over. Yes, you must stay a little later also. It just looks good. Take those five minutes to decompress from the workday and prepare to get into traffic. If you stay five minutes later, you will have at least three minutes with your supervisor alone. He or she may be willing to share exclusive information with you while you see your co-workers fly out of the office. Although your co-workers won't be doing anything wrong, it is really all about perception.

Habit #2: Prepare to Perform

An important habit to form is making a daily to-do-list before you begin working. It's a best practice that allows you to stay on task and keep up with all of the work you have to complete. In addition, it allows for you to carefully document what you have completed.

Start your day with a to-do-list and use your list from the previous day(s) to prioritize what is important today. When you create a to-do list and use it faithfully, it will be easier for you to document your tasks and accomplishments when asked. Most companies will require you to complete a weekly report. But if not, do a weekly report anyway. Jot down your completed tasks each day and create a weekly report at the end of each week.

Documenting your performance will save you the headache during evaluation time. During an annual/biannually/quarterly evaluation (however your organization has decided to evaluate), your supervisor will require you to list out all of your accomplishments and goals. You must be able to clearly prove your performance if you would like to keep your job. Having weekly reports will also serve as great documentation when it comes time to request a salary increase or when you are preparing your resume to move forward.

I also recommend that you keep a copy of your time card or the exact time you sit down at your desk. Although I would love for each of us to have wonderful bosses, the odds of any of us having *only* good bosses is slim to none. However, if you get in the habit and you carefully document your daily tasks and your time, it is hard for even a difficult boss to not see your dedication.

I always tell my clients to keep a workbook. Record your daily tasks, daily time in and out, and anything that happens during the day. Keeping a good record in your workbook will require a daily commitment. It is always great to write in your workbook when you first get to work (after all, you're getting there at least five to ten minutes early now!) and take that same five minutes at the end of your day and write in your workbook before you leave. It may be for your own personal record keeping use, like tracking data from the same time last year, or it may be to protect yourself later. Then, all you have to do is whip that bad boy out and rest your case.

You can thank me later.

This will only take ten minutes out of your day, but having mental clarity and clear documentation when shit goes down will mean everything!

Habit #3: Every day is Training Day

As a young professional, you are ultimately in charge of your own professional development. No one is going to make you read. No one is going to make you pay for training, certifications, or keep up with what is going on in your industry. You are in charge of how far your dreams will go, and if you want to be an executive or a high paying professional I am here to tell you that you must train every single day.

It is very important for you to stay up to date on current trends in your industry, movers and shakers in your industry, cutting-edge technology, and other resources. The only way you can really train every day is by reading everything that is available to you in your industry. Reading is the foundation to your promotion and you must get into a daily habit of reading.

Think about it like this. Let's say you get sick and you go to the nearest urgent care because you are vomiting and have a fever. You walk into the doctor's office, pay whatever they ask you to pay, and sit down waiting for your name to be called. The nurse comes to get you, takes your vital signs, and tells you the doctor will be in shortly. When the doctor finally comes in, he immediately tells you will need a shot and probably some medication. The nurse returns, and what if she tells you she hasn't given a shot to someone in about four years and she is really scared to administer the shot? I bet you that you would be ready to walk right out of that office.

Just like we require our health care professionals, hair stylists, auto technicians, chefs, to stay up to date on their certifications and skill set, we must do the same.

I suggest that you take 60 minutes each day and read about anything in your industry. Be sure the information is scholarly and from a source you can trust. Almost all industries out there have some type of virtual subscription you can pay for, and I promise you it will be worth it. The more you read, the more you will know. The more you are able to talk big-picture, technology, industry trends with professionals, the better conversations you will be able to have with your colleagues and role models.

Better conversations lead to speaking engagements, job opportunities, article features. All the fun stuff. Take time to develop a habit of reading each day. It is the least you can do for your professional growth.

Habit #4: Listen more than you talk

As an entry-level professional, you will be filled with many ideas and suggestions that you will want to share with your colleagues, your bosses, your mentors. Wait it out though. You must be able to show you can handle simple tasks and have a general understanding of the basics before you decide to share your opinion. In other words, you need to crawl before you walk.

You were taught to use a pencil before you were given an opportunity to use a pen. You sit in class and listen before the professor and do some readings before he asks you to present. With everything there comes a process of growth, and in the workplace you should listen first and talk in private later. Trust me, I learned this the hard way.

I worked for a company and I was asked to sit in on

a meeting with a non-profit organization that was looking to gain support from my company. There were three of us board members, and we were tasked with brainstorming ways to get the employees involved with donating.

Well, I listened first and just smiled. I'll be honest, I already knew they were only talking fluff, so I just listened. When they had all dried up and noticed I had said nothing, the room got quiet and they asked me what I thought they should do.

I told them what needed to be done and I gave solutions right down to the best time they should do it. I left the boardroom feeling electrified and rejuvenated. My company gave me the opportunity to talk and it was amazing! Two months later I had an evaluation meeting with my boss, and if you didn't already guess, she brought it up.

She said, "Chandria, you are doing wonderful. We love your energy and your enthusiasm."

But then the conversation turned.

She sarcastically added, "You must want to do my job!"

I was taken aback, but feigned a laugh and replied, "No! I love what I do."

At the end of the conversation, she told me that I was wrong for speaking out in the meeting. She looked me straight in the face and said, "If you are not an expert on the topic, you should not speak on it."

I thought to myself, "Lady, I was asked to attend this meeting and they asked me what I thought!"

She continued to say, "If you had ideas, you should have run them by senior leadership when the meeting was over."

As confused as you are, I was times a thousand. But I am not now.

Even if you know the answer, most seniors would prefer you not say it without their consent. This is especially true if you are new. I'm not saying you shouldn't have an opinion, but you must be sure it is suitable for the situation. When you are in a meeting, when you are in a training, when you are having casual conversation with your co-workers, be sure to listen before you speak.

You will learn a lot about the office, the dynamics, peoples personalities and most importantly, each person's craziness. I'm not saying what happened was right. I finally understand, after two years, the way meetings work!

Make it a habit to listen harder than you want to speak and eventually, people will give you the floor. Another great way for your voice to be heard is to mention your thoughts and ideas to your leadership after a meeting where it was being discussed. Don't send an email, catch him or her and ask if they have five minutes to discuss an idea you had. Once you are able to show both your loyalty and respect, and your wisdom, pretty soon you will be the one leading meetings!

But first, sit back and listen to what your leadership and colleagues are saying. Bring your workbook, record and review the meeting notes, and offer your advice during a one-on-one meeting later.

If you have a great boss, at the next meeting he or she will specifically ask you to share with the team what you shared in private. That is when you will know you have made an impression on your senior leadership.

Forming these four habits will take you some time and practice. None of us get it right the first time, but since you know what is expected of you, you can begin now working on your habits. If you practice these four habits right and often, you won't need to practice them any longer. They will be a part of your day and everything will go as planned. You will be leading the meetings and presentations with a workbook that will soon allow you to advocate for the raise of your dreams, and you will have a team that respects your intelligence.

Those ten extra minutes it takes to come in a little early and leave a little later will pay off, too. If it helps you to become the next favored employee trust me, there are perks!

TO-DO LIST

Use this space to start making your to-do lists, weekly reports, and workbook. Record your daily activities, how much time you spend on each task, and when you clock in and out each day. Once you fill up the page, start a new workbook for your activities!

10

YOU HAVE TO KEEP IT NOW

I have a client who reached out to me about six months ago seeking a promotion. He was tired of his current job and wanted a new start. This particular client was very skilled in project management and had worked as a project manager for a car company for almost two years.

Looking for a new beginning, he put me on retainer and began career coaching. Within less than a month, he was hired as a project manager with an amazing company. They offered him a salary that was $5,000 more than what he had been paid at his former position, and all was well. However, just two weeks ago, this same client called me with some bad news. He had been fired. After just six months on the job, they let him go.

I couldn't believe it! He was an amazing Project

Manager with great communication skills, was a great team player, and an innovative thinker. I could not imagine how he had been let go so quickly. So I asked. I asked him why they let him go, and you wouldn't believe what he said.

He got fired because of punctuality! Showing up to work late! He was already bummed and the damage had been done, so I didn't lecture him. But I could not believe he lost a near six-figure income because of something as silly as punctuality.

On our next call, he went into a little more detail. As it turns out, this new company he had joined used a point system for tracking work infractions. If you are late for so many days to your job, your late days turn into full day absences! Even five minutes late was crucial timing and counted against him! He admitted that at his last project management position, they regularly went into work late and no one said anything. So this bad habit continued in his new workplace. Many professionals think landing a job opportunity is actually the hardest part, but research and high turnover show keeping a job may actually be harder than landing one!

Research has shown that for millenials, the Top 5 Unacceptable behaviors companies are not willing to put up with are...

. . .

#1. Integrity Issues
   #2. Absences/Punctuality
   #3. Poor Performance
   #4. Unprofessional habits
   #5. Social Media Non-Sense

#1. Integrity Issues

It is easier to just tell the truth than to wait until someone brings up the issue. I know a young lady who was let go because she failed to tell her boss the truth before things went bad. This particular client was working on a major finance case and her boss asked her to email the client investment information that was very time sensitive. She agreed to get the information to their client by noon and she continued working on a previous assignment.

Noon came and went, and she forgot to send the time-sensitive paperwork to their client. Days went by, the client never saw the time-sensitive paperwork, and it wasn't until the boss didn't get paid from the sale when they noticed the paperwork wasn't sent out. When the commission report was reviewed, the client was not on it and the boss asked his employee what happened.

She lied! She told the boss she sent the paperwork and the client forgot to send it back. Email receipts served proof that the employee lied, and she was fired 30 minutes later! Telling the truth, even if there are consequences, is the most important character trait you must have. Integrity is everything! Not only can companies lose customers, but they can also lose lawsuits, malpractice cases and their entire business. Be sure to understand exactly what is expected of you each day.

If you have any questions, please ask someone and tell the truth. The best way to maintain integrity is to do what you say you are going to do, when you agree to do it. Anytime you are assigned a project, ask for a deadline. Write your deadline on your calendar and be sure to turn your work in before it is scheduled to be submitted.

Never start a project without asking for adequate implementation time and a reasonable deadline; unless your supervisor is demanding a report or information right now, there is always a time they are expected to receive the information back by. Requesting a timeline allows you to understand how much time you have to complete the project and makes sure that you and your supervisor are on the same page.

Most people who are promoted from one opportunity to the next are promoted because they are organized and extremely sensitive to deadlines. They possess integrity and don't mind informing their supervisor if a project will be behind normal schedule. If you want a promotion, practice integrity each day by requesting for deadlines. Be upfront and honest about commitments and do exactly what is expected of you in a timely manner!

#2: Absences/Punctuality

Time is money! When you are scheduled to be at work, you have contracted your services to perform for your company from the time you are scheduled to work until the time you are scheduled to leave. When you are not at work during your scheduled time, you are not only reneging on your job description, but you are also losing the company money and productivity.

No matter how nice your boss may be, it's always good to form a habit of coming to work on time and leaving work on time! I didn't ask you to stay late, although it is okay to stay late or come in early if your job requires it for a certain project. But 90% of your work schedule should be timed accordingly.

One of my work-study students who I love dearly always came to work at least five minutes late. When I offered constructive feedback on his punctuality, his response was "Five minutes, Mrs. Harris!"

Yes, five minutes! Because five minutes will turn into ten minutes and ten minutes will turn into thirty.

When an employee is dependable, it means everything to the employer. They can count on you to come to work on time and get the job done. You may think this isn't an issue but trust me, most people show up to work when they want to, take long lunches and have the nerve to ask to leave five minutes early to pick up their pets or volunteer for a community service project.

Just like my client's employer, some companies may have formal systems in place for tardiness. It will be extremely hard to explain to a recruiter or company you are interested in that you were fired from your last position because of punctuality.

Most companies will have a formal process to request time off from work. Be sure to shy away from asking for time off from work within your 90 days of employment. Asking for time off in your 90 days without discussing the time needed during your interview is extremely distasteful and will definitely throw up a red flag.

That said, life happens sometimes and you must take time off. If an emergency takes place during your 90 days, be sure to share it with your supervisor, attempt to make up the time and thank them for allowing you to not be at work.

I had a student who was assigned to an amazing marketing internship opportunity during the summer. Although the student didn't think it was important to tell me, her previous supervisor emailed me a long message to inform me that she'd let my student go.

Her email read, "Kate has failed to return my calls or come to work. I thought something may be wrong with her or her family, so we tried calling her on one of my employee's cell phone. She answered, laughed, and said she wasn't coming back."

It is really hard for me to say Kate was fired because of a phone call. It seemed like she just quit. Whatever you do, don't be Kate! If you are unhappy with your position, be sure to share that information with someone and if things don't change, turn in the appropriate two weeks notice.

You are considered a professional now and you must do professional things in order to salvage current relationships. Oftentimes, young professionals think it is okay to quit a job without notice. But it is not. It's way too early in your career to burn big bridges like that.

#3. Poor Performance

From not coming to work on time, to coming to work and doing the bare minimum, companies do not have time for poor behavior from employees. Trust me, these issues will be an almost immediate ticket out the door.

When you are hired to do a particular job, you are hired to solve a problem. You're expected to be the solution, help the team, and when you decide you are going to do the bare minimum, you renege on your agreed responsibilities.

Even if the job turns out to be not what you wanted or expected, perform to your best! Everything you do will be seen or heard about, while you work for the company and when you decide to give notice. Your work performance will be wrapped all up in the legacy you would like to leave at the company. People talk and the very person you think may never find out, will be connected some way to the next position you want to go afterwards.

I had a student stop by my office last year, dressed to impress with a very nice resume. I was so ecstatic to see a potential work-study student who understood what I wanted.

We sat down and talked for a couple of minutes and then I told her I'd be in touch. Excited, I went to my colleague's office and told them about this potential work-study student. My colleague looked at me with a deep concern and as her face grew to be rosier and rosier, she said no ma'am! That guy is a scam. He will smooth-talk his way into anything. He knows how to dress, he has a great resume, but he hardly does any work.

Shocked, I asked, "Really, how do you know him"?

She told me he was once hired as an intern for a company where her sister was an HR manager. He complained a lot about certain tasks and he wasn't a good team player. I was pretty disappointed with the news, but I have so much respect for my colleague who was courageous enough to keep me away from low-performing employees.

. . .

Sure, perhaps this guy could have learned his lesson and was back on the straight and narrow ready to achieve his career dreams and now an opportunity he almost had was turned down because of poor performance a year ago.

Let me just say this, I am a woman of second chances and I absolutely love to help students and young professionals, however, I trust my colleague's word over the student's potential. I didn't have time to correct his past or look more into his work ethics. This is the perfect case scenario of why performing at your best, and being truthful about opportunities will always help more than it will hurt anything!

There are five important behaviors you should do to exercise good habits of a top performer.

#1. Write down every assignment given. If your supervisor requests something of you in passing, go ahead make a mental note and formalize the project implementation time in email.

#2. Be resourceful. Don't ever expect anyone to know everything! Ask great questions but also listen very carefully. If you listen carefully you will learn buzzwords, systems, things you can go and research more! Be the person who has the answer and can solve complex problems. You will gain lots of work relationships from being resourceful and a person someone can call on about anything in your department or your company.

#3. Never complain! As bad as your work responsibilities can be, don't complain about it! Do what is required of you to get the job done and begin searching for new opportunities inside or outside the company. When someone asks you how things are going, unless you trust them with caring for your child, don't say anything negative. Stay positive, stay pleasant, and stay ready for opportunities ahead.

#4. In order to perform, you must come to work, understand your assignments, and practice integrity! You will be amazed by how many employees in the company take a liking to you simply because you do your work and remain uncomplicated. Which brings me to my next point.

#5. Avoid unprofessional work habits. As tempting as it may be to discuss things that are going on in your department, please don't. Keep your mouth closed, unless it is a mandatory statement. Gossip forms in the most unintentional ways and even if you have a good heart and a great deal of concern about a situation, everything that needs to be said, doesn't have to be said by you. Take it from me and one of my early mess-ups.

THERE WAS MORE to the story of my first board meeting. I was in a board meeting with my only other coworker and external partners discussing innovative ways to get employees to donate to a non-profit cause. I knew better than to say anything negative during the meeting, so I just sat there, smiled, and waited to be called on. After they discussed their ideas, they asked my opinion.

Although I praised their ideas, I offered up three more ideas to add to the conversation. When my supervisor asked me how the meeting went, because she didn't attend the meeting, I told her everything was okay, and I was hopeful we would choose the best idea for the company. She asked me what was my least favorite and I told her.

My boss later told my colleague what I said. It was a mess! She was near tears because I didn't think her idea was good enough.

Now trust me, this was way over my head and I had no clue why my supervisor would tell her I didn't like the idea and why she would care that a new person didn't like it. I was raised that if you don't like something, say it. A closed mouth doesn't get fed, but boy that doesn't translate properly in the workplace.

I didn't get fired for the incident, but I never fixed my relationship with the other employee.

Here are some other unprofessional work habits you should be aware of:

. . .

- Don't warm up fish in the microwave! No one wants to smell your lunch. Save your fish for home and bring something more pleasantly aromatic! Your coworkers will thank you for this courtesy.
- Be cognizant of other scent sensitivities. Too much cologne can make the workspace difficult for others.
- Loud talking, loud laughing, and always joking are also a "No-no". Please have a great time at work, but be sure to use your inside voice.
- Excuses don't pay the bills or positively affect your performance. If you are an employee who usually comes up with a lot of them, trust me, your teammates are sick of your excuses. Be accountable for your actions and shy away from blaming everything on everybody else.
- Misuse of emails and cc'ing people for no reason! Please don't blind copy anyone. I learned this the hard way too. My boss asked me to send someone an email and I thought it would be cute to blind copy my boss on the email so that he can see I sent it. It was definitely the wrong thing to do. He came into my office and asked me how often I blind copied others on emails and he would much prefer if I would have just cc'd (copied) him on the email. It looks sneaky and very unprofessional!

. . .

Honestly, this chapter makes it seem like you can be fired for sneezing wrong at work. My goal isn't to scare you and make you feel like you can't be yourself in the workplace, but to encourage you to be your professional self at work. Everybody shouldn't be privy to the personal side of your life unless they earn the right to see it.

I absolutely love and hate social media all at the same time. There are so many rewarding perks like connecting with the coolest professionals across the world. The access, visibility, and unlimited opportunities to make a name for yourself is unparalleled to the access other generations had. Now, awful but funny work memes are very common among social media posts I see on a daily basis. They are funny and full of humor, but the message itself is reflective on how you feel about your job.If you use social media the correct way, you expand your opportunities to be seen by some amazing people. But if you use social media the wrong way, the cons are so intensive and could be deadly to your marriage, friendships, and your career!

I was watching the news a couple days ago and overheard this funny but awful story about a daycare worker who was fired because of her social media post. She posted on Facebook, "I hate children" with a picture of her frowning and pouting about working. Well, her supervisor caught word of her post from parents she had added as friends on Facebook and she was fired on the spot! She was extremely upset, disturbed the peace, the police were called and then she showed up on the 6 o'clock news because of a Facebook post she said she didn't really mean! Word from the wise, "Please watch what you put on Facebook".

There are a couple of Facebook unprofessional habits you should be aware of:

- Monitor your actual social media posts. Anytime you make a social media post be sure you would be okay with the whole world seeing your post forever. If you think you can delete a post and it's gone forever, you are wrong! The Library of Congress houses every single tweet, post, hashtag, you name it... it can be pulled.

- Check your privacy settings and consider monitoring your tags and shares. I know we all have some very crazy cousins, uncles, and friends. Although you may want to laugh at their post, look at your page. Don't allow them to have free will to post whatever they would like on your page. Especially if you are in the midst of a job search!

- Register under an alias name. You may get away with freedom of speech on the web this way, but keep in mind, if someone ever tags you in a post and use your real name, you can be googled, and your page will pop up. Also, large companies may request password access to your social media accounts as a stress test during an interview. Be prepared to comply if they really decide to check it!

Sneezing at work won't get you fired, but unprofessional workplace habits will definitely send you walking.

    Watch your words,
watch your social media,
come to work on time,
Then work hard and play later!

Take inventory of your current habits. What will benefit you in the workplace, and what will be detrimental? Do you have trouble arriving on time? Do you easily get distracted by social media? List those habits below, and brainstorm some ways to help you break free of them!

11

SUCCEEDING WITH GRACE

There is so much pressure to make the right career decision and get it right the first time that it is almost crippling. The stakes are high, your family and friends are watching, and it is mentally tough to feel like you are operating under that kind of pressure. This has happened to me too. I remember my final semester leading up to graduating with my master's degree in Counseling and Psychology, I received the news I had failed my comprehensive exam. At the time, it was the most embarrassing situations I had to endure. I felt incompetent, inadequate and the thought of sharing the information with my husband and family was extremely stressful.

I finally muscled up the strength to tell them I had to retake my exam and I may walk the following semester (December). I was so heartbroken that I didn't succeed the first time that when I actually passed the exam, I decided I didn't want to walk across the stage. I thought it would be best to just have the degree mailed to me and to move on with my life. This one roadblock not only crushed me, but made me bitter.

We hear it all the time. "If at first you don't succeed, try again!" and it sounds amazing until you have to be the one to do it and to try again in front of everyone! It wasn't until my husband sat me down and forced me to unpack why I didn't want to attend the graduation ceremony that I was able to get to the heart of my disappointment. At first, I pouted about how the university was too far to travel to. (I was completing my master's online). He silenced the lie by pointing out that the university is four hours away from us. After 30 minutes of talking through why I didn't want to walk any longer, we finally landed on the truth. My ego. My pride. I didn't want to participate in the graduation ceremony because I was still torn up about not passing my first comprehensive exam and I felt ashamed.

The story ends beautifully. I decided to participate in the graduation ceremony and it was a wonderful feeling to tell the story of how hard I worked to hold my master's degree. Because here's the thing about ego and pride - we believe looking perfect is admired and celebrated and in reality, we as humans enjoy hearing more about the journey, the resilience, the story of endurance because this is what happens to most of us in real life. The pain I felt was self-inflicted. In reality, my community celebrated my achievement because of the persistence I embodied to move forward.

Many times we feel it is important to be perfect, to get it right the first time and to show up without any flaws. The truth is that your ability to succeed beyond adversity is far more important in life and in the workplace. Our perspectives, insights, systems, processes come from our experiences and journey. It is what makes us unique and brilliant. It is exactly what hiring managers, decision makers, your family, your friends, your community would like to hear. They want to see your ability to overcome and succeed because it will ultimately forecast how you will show up for them in their life trials and how you will perform in the workplace when the work is full of obstacles and challenges. Having a big ego and being prideful are two detrimental character flaws that mentally and physically cripple opportunities to gain insight, clarity and awareness. So let us push our ego and pride to be perfect to the side and in every opportunity show up our best.

At any moment on your journey, you'll start to ask yourself what others will say about you and your decisions. You'll think to yourself, "How will I look to my friends and family if this doesn't work out? I have to look right no matter what." When this happens, I challenge you to check your ego. These questions are sure signs of a desire to show up perfect but, no one is asking you to be perfect but yourself. The pressure that you are feeling is self-deprecating.

Now what others *are* expecting of you is your absolute best. Being your best requires you to know what is expected of you and to go out for it steadfastly in your research and savviness. When you are looking to reach a goal, it is important to be very familiar with the expectations and outlined factors for success. When you are aware of what is required, you are able to take the necessary steps to achieve those things.

As an example: If you are interested in being an entrepreneur and owning a business, the best way to run a business is to learn from others who are doing it well. This will require you to find a mentor, shadow and even work full-time supporting various functions of the business that will help you bypass many of the obstacles you would probably endure without the lessons of others. Your ego may say, "Do it alone. You've got it. You will make mistakes, but you don't need to work for someone to be successful." WRONG!

The prerequisite to being the best at what you do is understanding how to do it well by connecting with industry leaders and not pretending to be the best already, but being prepared to put in the work to learn how it is done. And yes, while you will learn a great deal from industry leaders, you will still meet with failure in the process that will allow you to flex your endurance and persistence muscles. And that's okay.

It is important to train your mind to think like a business professional and ultimate winner.

The best way to begin to train your mind is:

#1. Understanding that being perfect is not what others are requiring, it's you.

#2. Becoming competent and knowledgeable in the work that interests and serves you is always best practice. Please don't fake it until you make it. This ideal and myth will have you mentally spiraling out of control and prompt you to lean into your pride and ego.

#3. Realizing you will need the help of others and their guided feedback (not always positive) to help you excel in life and in business.

#4. Taking baby steps as you begin to strengthen your persistence muscle. Set a goal to wake up every morning by 6:00 a.m. for 30 days. Weekends, birthdays, special events, don't matter. Try your best to be up and out of bed at 6:00 a.m. Write down what you say to yourself every day as the alarm goes off. Hear the motivation or minimizing thoughts and push through them. Feel the pain your body drums up as you embrace this difference and be reminded that this step is a trial run for you setting a goal to achieve. There will be days you will identify every reason to not get out of bed, and you must push through that. There will be days you deserve to lay down five extra minutes, please push through that. There will be moments you will begin to mentally prepare the night before for reasons why you should stop this goal because you have nothing to do the next day, push through this too. Journal every day, every thought around your new goal. When your 30 days comes to an end, reflect on each note. Compare and contrast your emotions and thoughts each day and reflect. This exercise is a wonderful technique to build upon and add new goals.

On this journey to discovering your life and career you will be approached by situations and obstacles that will give you every reason to give up. Your ego, pride and the thoughts of others are the biggest influences that will and can get in the way of you achieving your goals. Challenge your thoughts and have exclusive conversations with your community and ask them about their goals and dreams. Ask them what hindered their success and ask why they didn't keep going. You will hear every excuse in the world that will equal to, "I didn't want to be seen as a failure to other people. I didn't want to let my family down. I didn't want to invest so much money and time because I have a family to take care of." Underneath each, you will hear EGO and PRIDE because being seen is a bit painful and crippling. Nothing - and I mean nothing - hurts more than really wanting to achieve something as the time to do it passes you by.

There are some things you will want to achieve in your career/life that are specifically bound to time, like running for homecoming queen, becoming drum major, competing in a competition, applying for a scholarship, applying for a grant. While we are able to make up for lost times by participating in other things, some of your goals will be bound in time and will require you to act now.

Don't allow your ego and pride to hinder you from acting now. Don't allow your ego and pride to stop you from asking the formal person in the position, competition, role for advice or tips. Don't allow your ego and pride to stop you from announcing it to the world (when it's time to do so) that you are chasing what you want.

Remember, we want to see you try your hardest and we ultimately want to see you win too, when that time comes.

Last Exercise

Take this inventory often to assess if you are allowing pride and your ego to get in the way of your goals and dreams.

1. Do you listen thoroughly when someone is teaching - even if it is a subject you are already familiar with?

2. Do you find certain tasks to be beneath you (classroom, work, internship, volunteering)? Being humble and doing good work will advance you.

3. Have you ever decided not to ask for help even when deep down you know you need it?

4. Do you aggressively share your ideas and opinions or always want to be the facilitator or teacher? Do you find yourself wanting to speak first all the

THE NOT SO BUTTONED-UP APPROACH

time, or often find others didn't say things the "right way"?

5. Do you look down on others by identifying ways you think you are better than them?

6. Do you disregard advice from other peers, professors, and other people who may be as knowledgeable or more knowledgeable on a topic than you aew?

7. Are you critical and always judging others? (This may be the reason why you fear others will judge you).

8. Do you struggle with accepting feedback and critiques? (For example, do you feel there is always a reason for something going wrong that is not you, or your responsibility?).

9. Do you have a disregard for leadership when not in leadership? Do you catch yourself thinking, "I can run this better than what they are doing?"

10. Are you a name-dropper? Do you feel like everyone needs to know you are connected to the highest-ranked professionals in your industry?

If you find yourself answering yes/true to one of these items, I suggest you begin to work on your ego and pride. There is no place for success when you are operating out of the belief that you are more than and better than others. Here is the good news, though: If you humble yourself and decide you no longer want to show up like this, you have taken the first step to accelerating your success. The new energy you will bring to every conversation and encounter will be filled with gratitude, love and an ear to learn. I believe in you and your growth and if you are feeling some discomfort, distressed or called out after this chapter, lean into it. Acknowledge the growing pains and do better.

12

YOU HAVE ARRIVED

"Ships at a distance have every man's wish on board. For some they come in with the tide. For others they sail forever on the same horizon, never out of sight, never landing until the Watcher turns his eyes away in resignation, his dreams mocked to death by Time." - Zora Neale Hurston

ZORA NEALE HURSTON wrote this meaningful quote in her book *Their Eyes were Watching God*. I truly believe we all have opportunities to go on, do great things, and achieve the life of our dreams. It is human wishes that prompt us to create goals. It is human wishes (the "why") that propels us to use the current, the wave, and the water to carry us to shore. This explains that, while all others are still in the water sailing, your ship has made its way to shore. You have arrived. Now what are you going to do?

When I think of the ocean's current, the waves, and the water that author Zora Neale Hurston refers to in *Their Eyes Were Watching God*, I use it to describe the situations, circumstances, and oftentimes the bad breaks that keep the ambitious people focused and driven to make it to their destination, despite the difficulty. All hell can break loose during the happiest times in your life. When you have finally earned the degree. When you have finally earned the certification. When you finally stopped living paycheck to paycheck. It always seems that that is when things turn for the worst. But don't fret! I truly believe that this actually means you are on the right track.

You have arrived despite making it through some trials and tribulations. However, you must still follow your faith during frustrating times. Laugh and learn from your lost L's and have audacity and determination.

As a little girl, my pastor and church choir sang soulful songs. There is one particular song that says, "Don't let the stumbling blocks stop your faith". The verse begins, "Trouble in my way, I have to cry sometimes." I vividly remember the church choir and members singing their hearts out, while I envisioned literal rocks stumbling down a wall, coming to attack me. Ever since then, Chan and big rocks don't mix.- Something so large, hard, and heavy, falling speedily towards me? I can't think of anything worse.

My Dad calls these stumbling blocks "situations and circumstances." I've asked him many times, "Why didn't you make it to the pharmacy before they closed?" or "Why did you cancel your doctor's appointment" or "Why are you just starting to cook Thanksgiving dinner at 3:30 p.m. on Thanksgiving Day?"

His response is always, "Situations and circumstances got in the way."

When you are embarking on a new journey in life, situations and circumstances will come, but you must be ambitious enough to not allow them to deter you from your faith and your focus. You must use your latest success of making it to shore, making it through school, making it through other trying times, to empower you to make it through the highs and lows of seeking and landing your dream job.

"Situation and circumstances," "stumbling blocks", or "the Jump-Man." It seems like when you are on the right path, something always comes up to get you off track.

My now husband, then boyfriend (the B.B. King fan), asked me to follow him to St. Louis, Missouri as he prepared to become a Licensed Financial Advisor. In order for him to become a Financial Advisor, he had to take two extremely hard tests. He passed one test before we left Mississippi, which is how the company offered for him to come up to St. Louis to begin work, while he studied to take the second and final test.

This second test was much tougher than he had ever anticipated. Although he is extremely smart and had prepared for this test for months, he failed on his first attempt. Without the passing grade, the company he was working for lapsed his job. We were recent graduates, in St. Louis, away from family, and my boyfriend had lost his job.

However, determined to pass the test, my husband continued to study, and he refused to give up. He told me, "I came to St. Louis to be a financial advisor and I will leave here a financial advisor."

He had faith that he would get through the test. So much faith that he actually proposed to me the day before his exam. He told me later that this moment of happiness, planning and executing an elaborate proposal and me saying "Yes!" gave him the energy and enthusiasm he needed to take the test. The next morning, he got up, put on his clothes, kissed me and headed to his exam site. I prayed and prayed until I got a call from him. When I heard his voice, everything in me knew he had passed that exam. And I was correct. He had passed!

Having faith during a frustrating time, when the Jump Man is out to get you, or your path looks full of stumbling blocks, gives you strength to abandon your worries and fears to someone more powerful and bigger than you. Once you have answered your calling, put in the work, connected with amazing people, have

THE NOT SO BUTTONED-UP APPROACH

full faith in your abilities, it is time to leave everything else to the powers that be.

The Jump Man doesn't come until everything is running Kosher, you see. The Jump Man is a test of courage, a test of strength, a test of versatility when things seem to be going well. Some of your best days will be hit with some craziness, but the true test is whether you will permit the stumbling blocks, the waves, and the current to get in your way... or will you conquer your biggest battle just as my husband did.

In the mornings, I always take time to call my mom. One particular morning, I woke up in a very good mood, got dressed, and was heading into work on time. My mom asked me how my morning was going and I had the nerve to say, "This day couldn't get any better." I got out of the car in my cute and classy black dress, nice new sheers, and a fresh pair of black pumps with my lunch in one hand and my cell phone in the other. Step by step, I strutted to my office.

As I touched the last outdoor step, I looked up and the next thing I knew, I was on the ground. I fell. Straight on my ass. In my pretty black dress, outside in the parking lot, directly in front of the most frequented building on campus. I jumped up quickly, smiled, and said to myself as I thought of my dad, "Well, that's a stumbling block!"

I wiped my sheers off, walked into my office as if nothing had happened, and I finally laughed! I laughed so hard...because who am I to be above falling? Who am I to be above missing a step? This is important because as you enter this journey, you will encounter these missteps too. You too will question yourself and say, "How did I make such a fool of myself?" or "Why me?" But you must ask yourself how you are above falling. Winston Churchill once said, "if you're going through hell, keep going," and I must agree with him.

You have to understand, those stumbling blocks, the Jump Man, whatever you want to call it… they don't come until everything is running Kosher. The Jump Man is a test of courage, a test of strength, and a test of versatility.

Let me share another story. I got married in 2016. The year before my wedding was my year of Situations & Circumstances. I remember being three weeks into a new job, preparing to interview to go onto the TV Show, Say Yes to the Dress. I was entering a very exciting time in my life! I really, really wanted to be on Say Yes To The Dress and I was just five minutes away from skyping the casting director when I clicked on Facebook and saw a post that changed my life.

My little sister had just posted, "I only have one grandmother left, please do not take my grandmother away."

My heart started to beat rapidly, so I closed the door and began to sob. I sobbed so violently, that I thought I would never get it together in time for my Skype call. The next thing I knew, instead of calling my parents I was answering a call from Kristi with Say Yes

To The Dress. I took a deep breath, muscled up all my strength, courage, my usually happy personality and completed the interview. I didn't immediately know if I would get the chance to go onto the show or not, but in a weird way I was proud and impressed that I didn't allow this huge stumbling block, the potential loss of my only remaining grandmother, get in the way of me fulfilling the dreams I know she wanted me to have.

Well, as you would guess, the moment the call and moment of pride were over, I called home. Unfortunately, the news was true. My grandmother had suffered a stroke, and her brain was bleeding on all four sides. My uncle never told me why he didn't call earlier, but when I spoke to him, he told me to leave Nashville now and get home. They did not expect my grandmother to live.

Don't forget, I was the new person on the job.

Once again, the Jump Man doesn't come until everything is running Kosher. The Jump Man is a test of courage, a test of strength, a test of versatility.

And so it begins...

On your journey to a new life, new is what is unknown. New is what is scary and what can sometimes make you uncomfortable. The Jump Man could be the old you trying to get in the way of the new you. The Jump Man could be faith testing you, just as I was tested when my grandmother endured a stroke. The Jump Man could be right before a moment of humbleness, as I quickly came back to reality and picked myself up off the ground after 'Chan took a tumble.' The Jump Man could be any person, place, or thing that might get in your way and hinder your progress. Your Jump Man may look a little different from mine, but the thing to understand is something will happen, and you must be prepared to move forward.

Let me repeat that. Something will happen, and something must happen.

Rainy days will come. If we read the almanac forecast for next year and the farmers predicted no rain at all, imagine our world! The flowers, the trees, our health, our food would be close to, if not completely, nonexistent. As much as most of us hate rainy days, we must have them. They are necessary to flourish. The Jump Man is a rainy day. The Jump Man is ketchup on a white tee shirt before your presentation. The Jump Man is a necessary occurrence that transpires to help you think quicker, act quicker, behave better, or control your emotions. Whatever you need to be better, the Jump Man has a way to bring you growth!

The Jump Man doesn't come until everything is running Kosher you see. The Jump Man is a test of courage, a test of strength, a test of versatility when things seem to be going well.

Whether you call them stumbling blocks like my old Southern Baptist Choir or you can relate better to my Dad, who calls them "Situations & Circumstance," just understand trouble will sometimes try to get in your way on your journey to success.

But before you give up, take a look at how far you have already come. Look at your compelling story, look at how you have come out, even when you thought things would never work out. Before you decide to give up on this new career dream, think about everything it took for you to get where you are now. Think about your why! Think about your successes, and muscle up the strength to move forward.

I did. And I'm so glad I did. Not only did I achieve the career of my dreams, but I defied the traditions of my family. I added another level to our family history, I empowered my sisters, brothers, and friends to broaden their horizons, try new things, and achieve higher heights! Not only did I do this and try to make my ancestors proud, but I evolved into answering my higher leadership and work calling.

So now, it is time for you to decide.

When you decide to answer your higher leadership and work calling, you give yourself permission to create a sustainable life that is long lasting not just a quick trip with your friends across the country.

When you decide to answer your higher leadership and work calling, you give yourself permission to grow, share what you know and watch your world thank you for your contribution.

When you decide to answer your higher leadership and work calling, you give yourself permission to dream, to believe bigger than you and to see magic happen in your life.

When you decide to answer you higher leadership and work calling, you have decided to not only live life, but contribute to others' lives and then my friend, you have decided to allow money to flow to you abundantly!

You have arrived!

TESTIMONIALS

"In a society that has grown increasingly complex, the road to a solid career path has become far more difficult to navigate. If anyone can steer you toward your goals and dreams, Chandria Harris can not only do it, but can do it with the grace, elegance, and knowledge you must have to set off on the right foot. I have interviewed hundreds of candidates for a wide variety of careers and, believe me, if Chandria coached any of them, my job would have been so much simpler. Chandria's voice is one that should be listened to and learned from before you take those first steps in what may well be the most important decision of your life"

William Anthony

Three years down and more to go Chandria Harris has been a sight to witness. Along with her persistence, bubbly personality, strong sense of direction and passion for students, she has changed not only my life, but others for the better. Without Mrs. Harris, I would not be where I am today. With her knowledge, proper skill sets, resources and expertise, she assisted me in landing job opportunities, leadership positions and my most recent internship at the National Association for the Advancement of Colored People (NAACP), as a Legislative Assistant in Washington, D.C.

Chandria pushes you beyond your limits because she see the potential in you. I am lucky to have found her, but more college students need to be exposed to this type of greatness. She understands the millennials further than the eye can see. She understands our problems, the way we think, our insecurities, and our dreams all because she has been where we are and she can relate. The power Mrs. Harris possess is almost like a secret. She researched it, she discovered it, and now she wants to give back. I truly believe by giving Chandria

Harris a higher platform for people to hear and see her would not only benefit millennials, but benefit the Professional Career Field as well.

Hailee Bryant-Roye

A few years ago, after losing my job, I reached out to Chandria for help. I was in a place where I had given up on myself and the job search all together. When I contacted Chandria, I was extremely impressed. Not only was she professional, she was supportive, attentive and knowledgeable. She equipped me with tools that empowered me to be more confident in myself and in my skills. After meeting with Chandria, I applied to one particular job, I had previously applied for this position but was not successful. After applying a second time, I landed an interview, mastered the interview and was offered the position. The tools that Chandria gave me are definitely lifelong tools.

Meagan Butler

My years of knowing Chandria, she has been a great asset in the lives of a students. I happen to be one of those students. Throughout my experience at Tennessee State University, Chandria's expertise in career development and counseling enabled her to sift through many opportunities from employers and advise the perfect one for me. In doing so, she also helped me recognize my strengths and weaknesses in terms of interviewing, written and oral communication, and even creating the perfect resume. Taking the advice of Chandria, I have been able to survive many interviews and become a successful young professional. I currently work for one of the top health insurance companies and I wouldn't have gotten this far with Chandria's assistance. Beyond students landing the desired role in their chosen careers, she is very impactful in the lives of students' personal and professional growth.

Monique Miller

Because of Chandria I now have a new outlook on finding a job, and developing my career. Chandria helped me realize my true passion but just asking one simple question. What do you want to be remembered for? I never thought your career is something to be remembered for but then it clicked. You should love what you do, and if you love what you do you'll be great at it. If it had not been for Chandria I would still be working a job I got straight out of college instead of living my dream, having a career that's meaningful and guiding others to do the same.

Darion Banister

ACKNOWLEDGMENTS

To Samuel & William:

I'm usually involved in a million and one things and there has never been a time where you have said your career is too much. Samuel, thank you for being a champion of my career and the completion of this book. Writing and publishing a book while transitioning into parents was one of the hardest things we accomplished today. When I look at the success of this book, I say we did it. You have been my quiet strength, my level of reason and daily reminder of I can do anything. I'm forever grateful for you husband. Thank you. We did it.

To My Family:

My life is extra special because I have amazing people like you to experience it with. Thank you for providing me with the space and the freedom to fly and reach higher heights. The leadership skills you have imparted in my life has empowered me to be consistent, persistent, and resilient. Thank you so much for your love and the extra push to be great!

To Emma:

Publishing a book is harder than I thought and more rewarding than I could have ever imagined. None of this would have been possible without you Emma. I literally could not have done this without you. I have never met a person who is so willing to see someone else succeed. Thank you for your patience, your kindness, your can-do activity and for helping publish this book. You have forever changed my life and have shown me how to trust others with something so special. I am forever in debt to you for your contributions to The Not-So-Buttoned Up Approach. Thank you!

To Students:

To the thousands of students, I have coached and counseled over the last five years, thank you for giving me the confidence to create a guide for you. Your stories, situations, complex challenges and ambitious to elevate your career is what I thought about daily when I was too afraid to put the ink to paper. Thank you for giving me a reason to share my story and to do so boldly. My hope is for students to pick up this book and feel empowered to do something with a checklist to begin.

Finally, to all those who have been a part of my getting there: Alma Turner, Genette Robinson, Glenda Glover, Lisa Shackelford, Angela Payne, Charles Jennings, Kristen Kolb, Bill Anthony, Riley Wallace, Jamal Coleman, and Kelly Wilde. Thank You!

ABOUT THE AUTHOR

Described as a "lifter of people," our CEO and founder Chandria Harris utilizes a strategic and intuitive approach to guide clients out of their comfort zones while minimizing discomfort and amplifying desired results.

As an award-winning Global Career Development Consultant and speaker, Chandria's strategy hinges on her belief in people's ability to succeed beyond their adversities, challenges, and blind spots. Over the course of her career, she has:

• Helped **more than 300 professionals of color** authentically gain more access and exposure to career opportunities

• Coached **more than 20 business executives and Fortune 500 leaders** in deepening their understanding of themselves and their teams, including international training events

• Influenced a **40% increase internship placement** at Tennessee State University`

- Served as a trusted recruitment advisor to **more than 100 businesses** across manufacturing, healthcare, higher education, entrepreneurship, and the non-profit space, with top clients like Thor Industries and Emory University.

Chandria holds a bachelor's degree in Social Science from Mississippi University for Women, a master's degree in Counseling/Psychology from The University of West Alabama, and certifications from these world-renowned training programs:
- Diversity, Equity, and Inclusion – Cornell University,
- Global Career Development - Center for Credentialing and Education
- Career Services Provider - National Career Development Association
- Certified Professional Resume Writer - Professional Association for Resume Writers and Career Coaches
- Public Administration - Mississippi University for Women

Chandria is originally from Mississippi and has enjoyed life in Nashville for the past six years. She and her husband, Samuel, welcomed William Carter Harris to their family in 2019.

www.ingramcontent.com/pod-product-compliance
Lightning Source LLC
Chambersburg PA
CBHW060835220526
45466CB00003B/1111